FAULT LINES

Niladri Roy is a leading voice on how organizations survive and thrive in times of disruption. A strategist, educator, and advisor with more than three decades of experience, he has guided CXOs, boards, and leadership teams through the challenges of digital transformation, business model reinvention, and organizational change.

As Founder of The Digital Academy and Managing Partner at ßmorphosis, he works with enterprises across industries to build future-ready strategies and leadership capabilities. A former faculty member at the Infosys Leadership Institute and a Chartered Accountant, Niladri combines analytical rigour with practical insight drawn from consulting, corporate leadership, entrepreneurship, and academia.

His work explores the intersection of strategy, technology, governance, and leadership, helping organizations identify the hidden fault lines beneath success—and equipping leaders to anticipate disruption before it becomes a crisis.

Connect with Niladri:
LinkedIn: https://www.linkedin.com/in/niladriroy/
YouTube: https://www.youtube.com/@NiladriRoy_Digital
Instagram: https://www.instagram.com/niladri.neelabjo/

FAULT LINES

Leading Through India's Era of AI, Platforms, and Reinvention

NILADRI ROY

RUPA

Published by
Rupa Publications India Pvt. Ltd 2026
161-B/4, Gulmohar House,
Yusuf Sarai Community Centre,
New Delhi 110049

Sales centres
Bengaluru Chennai
Hyderabad Kolkata Mumbai

P-ISBN: 978-93-7957-555-5
E-ISBN: 978-93-7957-820-4

First impression 2026

10 9 8 7 6 5 4 3 2 1

Printed in India

To my father
Nishithendu Lal Roy (1935–2026)

He taught me discipline without rigidity,
resilience without complaint, and integrity without display.

The values he lived by continue to shape
how I think, how I work, and how I lead.
This book carries his imprint in ways
words cannot fully express.

Contents

Part Three
Foresight: Who's Next and Why

Part Four
India's Resilient Reinventors

Part Five
The Future: AI and the Next Platform Wave

Preface

I grew up in Kolkata between the mid-1970s and the early 1990s, in an India shaped by a quiet paradox—rich in imagination, yet restrained in ambition. Trams rattled past old colleges, the annual Book Fair felt like a festival of ideas and the Sunday evening movie on Doordarshan drew entire neighbourhoods into a shared moment. We were a country that prized self-reliance, shaped by the belief that the State would build national capability brick by brick. Businesses learned to grow within ceilings, consumers learned to navigate scarcity with patience, and talent learned to dream within boundaries.

For me, these memories are not nostalgia; they are reference points. They remind me how dramatically the ground beneath us has shifted thereafter.

Liberalization in 1991 did not replace one story with another—it loosened the rigid architecture of the old one. Slowly, we embraced competition, openness, and global benchmarks. Choice appeared where scarcity once lived. Indian companies encountered new expectations. Indian talent discovered new arenas.

And yet, the shift was not ideological so much as geological—slow, uneven, and layered. India was renegotiating its economic identity in real time, balancing welfare with aspiration, and state protection with entrepreneurial freedom.

Then, over the next two decades, something deeper unfolded—a reconstruction that rewired not just markets but behaviour itself. Aadhaar redefined identity. India Stack embedded trust, authentication, and consent into a digital backbone. The Jan Dhan–Aadhar–Mobile (JAM) trinity expanded financial inclusion at an unprecedented scale. Reliance Jio collapsed the cost of data and democratized access. UPI redrew the economics of payments. Platforms reorganized industry after industry. And now, artificial intelligence (AI) is accelerating that reorganization even further.

For someone who remembers adjusting rooftop antennas in Kolkata just to catch a faint foreign broadcast, these shifts feel nothing short of extraordinary. I remember the thrill of cable television arriving in our neighbourhood, the pride of seeing the first colour TV in a friend's home, and later, the intrigue of mobile phones as rare objects of privilege. When I entered the workforce in 1995, technology felt distant, almost ornamental.

Today, it is the infrastructure of everyday life.

A vegetable vendor in Ranchi accepts UPI.

A student in Coimbatore retrieves her marksheet on DigiLocker.

An entrepreneur in Guwahati completes e-KYC in minutes.

Millions consume global content on devices that fit in the palm.

In one generation, distance, documentation, hierarchy, and access have been reorganized.

This book is my attempt to make sense of that transformation—not as a chronology of technological achievements, but as a deeper story of how economics, politics, governance, identity, and behaviour have interacted to reshape Indian enterprise, and continue to do so.

In this book, I refer to these deeper forces as fault lines. Borrowing from geology, fault lines are fractures beneath the earth's surface where pressures accumulate long before they reshape the landscape above. Organizations are no different. Beneath periods of apparent stability, hidden tensions build and eventually surface as disruption. Chapter 6 explores this idea in detail. For now, it is enough to recognize that what appears sudden is often years in the making.

Why Leaders Must Understand India's Fault Lines

The disruptions shaping Indian business today often appear sudden, platforms scaling overnight, consumer behaviour shifting in months rather than years, and incumbents, or those entities that faced the challenge, losing ground in industries they once defined. Yet, when seen through the longer arc of India's economic and technological journey, these changes are not sudden at all. They are the predictable outcomes of structural movements—fault lines—that have been silently forming over decades.

This book argues that India's corporate failures are rarely the result of external shocks alone. More often, they emerge from internal mismatches between the following:

- speed of the market and that of the organization,
- behaviour of consumers and the assumptions of leadership, and
- architecture of the economy and the organization.

Understanding these mismatches—these fault lines—is not an academic exercise. It is the starting point for leadership in a country where disruption is not an exception but the norm.

What This Book Contains

This book is divided into five sections, each examining a different dimension of India's fault line economy.

Part I: India's Platform Era

This section traces the rise of India's digital public infrastructure and platform economy—from Aadhaar to UPI to Jio—to reveal how these systems created new markets, behaviours, and expectations. It shows that India's 'platform state' did not emerge by accident; it evolved through a series of deliberate choices that continue to redefine competitive dynamics.

Part II: The Three Fault Lines of Platform Disruption

This section examines companies such as Moser Baer, Zee, MTV India, HMT, and BSNL. These are not stories of failure, but of transition—how legacy formats eroded, governance gaps widened, and platforms displaced long-standing business models. Each case reveals a different fault line.

Part III: Foresight—Who's Next and Why

If Part II helps leaders understand why disruption happened, Part III helps them anticipate where it may happen next. It introduces a set of practical frameworks—the Fault Line Fragility Index™, the Early Signal Radar™, the Fault Line Disruption Dashboard™, and the Fault Line Maturity Model™—designed to help practising managers detect emerging vulnerabilities, interpret weak signs and assess their organization's readiness for change. In an environment where disruption often becomes visible only after it is too late, these tools offer leaders a structured way to ask better questions, challenge assumptions and act before fault lines widen into crises.

Part IV: India's Resilient Reinventors

This part looks at the companies that successfully transformed themselves by successfully navigating the fault lines—Reliance/

Jio, Tata Group, ICICI Bank, Titan, Marico, Infosys, HUL, and Indian Railways. Their journeys illustrate that agility is not a slogan but a deliberate outcome of how organizations design their governance, talent, technology, and decision-making. Reinvention is possible, but only when leaders acknowledge the fault lines beneath them.

Part V: The Future—AI and the Next Platform Wave

The final section looks ahead to the evolving architecture of the Indian economy—AI platforms, indigenous models, new forms of identity, and emerging governance structures. These projections are not certainties; they are offered to help leaders cultivate readiness rather than rely on prediction.

What This Book Ultimately Asks of the Reader

This is not a book of prescriptions; it is a book of perspectives.

My aim is not to be right in every prediction or interpretation. In fact, some of my ideas will inevitably be proven wrong—and that is entirely acceptable. The intention is to spark a way of thinking: to help leaders see patterns rather than isolated events, to recognize movements rather than moments.

Because leadership in India today demands more than strategy.

It requires the ability to read the shifting ground beneath one's feet, and that is pattern recognition overlayed with imagination.

I have lived through an India that has rebuilt itself more than once—sometimes slowly, sometimes dramatically. From an era of ration cards and regulated ambition to a world of platforms, AI, and billion-user digital infrastructure, I have watched the country redefine its possibilities. This book is both a reflection of that journey and a guide for those navigating its next chapter.

India is not only changing; it is changing the very terms on which change itself unfolds.

And those who understand its fault lines—its pressures, its accelerations, its peculiar rhythms—will help shape its future.

Part One

INDIA'S PLATFORM ERA

1

The Making of Digital India

India's first great shockwave—its escape from a state-controlled industrial economy into the unpredictability of a liberalized market—involved the unshackling of factories, where consumers discovered choice and businesses learned to compete rather than comply. However, liberalization merely laid the groundwork. The real rupture in India's economic story was yet to come.

The second shockwave, which turned India into one of the world's most dynamic platform economies, was bigger, deeper, and faster. It unfolded within a single generation.

This chapter tells that story, not as a chronology of events but as a narrative of inflection points. It explores moments when India's economic, technological, and social landscape accelerated, converged, and produced a digital infrastructure unlike any other in the world. At each juncture, something shifted fundamentally, whether it be behaviour, access, trust, speed, incentives or the architecture of the economy itself.

Individually, these shifts were significant. Together, they created the foundations of India's platform era, whose fault lines will shape every case study in this book.

The Foundation of a Digital Shift

Liberalization did not make India digital. It changed the mindset of an entire nation, setting the stage and preparing it for a transformation that would arrive years later.

From 1991 onwards, a few shifts began to take shape. The first was the arrival of choice, followed by the mobile revolution. Then, it was India's IT services industry, which was building the country's digital capability.

When India Discovered Choice

Through the 1990s, India went from being a scarcity-driven market to an explosion of choice. Satellite television replaced Doordarshan's monotony. Branded consumer goods arrived. Foreign products filled shelves. Organized retail began to take shape.

This was the first moment in modern India when consumer behaviour began shifting quickly and at scale.

I remember this shift not as an analyst but as an adolescent of the Doordarshan era. This was an India where entertainment arrived in rationed doses. On some evenings, when the clouds cooperated, our family's makeshift booster antenna would catch a faint signal from Bangladesh TV, and for 30 glorious minutes, I could watch *Knight Rider* through a haze of static. It felt like peeking into another world. Then, almost overnight, cable TV arrived. Dozens of channels, colours, stories, and music, choices that were previously unimaginable, burst into our living rooms. The same transformation unfolded in the markets with branded clothes and global labels. Even a pair of Levis no longer depended on an uncle returning from the United States. It was the first time I truly felt that India's moment had arrived and that the consumer was no longer a passive recipient but the king around whom the market orbited. Because when the value is clear, adoption is instant. This willingness to embrace new formats, brands, and consumption patterns would later define the speed at which India adopted digital platforms, that is, faster than most large nations, except maybe China.

The Mobile Revolution: From Luxury to Lifeline

I witnessed this change at close quarters. When I joined the workforce in 1995, fresh out of my chartered accountancy, mobile phones were mythical objects. They were rumoured, rare, and reserved for the upwardly mobile. In early 1996, I saw my first one: a bulky handheld contraption that a partner at our firm carried like a trophy. Incoming calls cost ₹12–13, an extravagance in those days, so he kept the device locked in his suitcase, terrified someone might accidentally use it.

A year later, when I moved to Oman, I bought my first mobile phone, a second-hand unit that fit my modest budget and felt nothing short of magical. By the time I returned to India in 1999, I could finally afford a sleeker, more fashionable handset. Incoming calls had become cheaper, and that phone became my lifeline, especially for the incessant conversations with Sona, my then-fiancée and now wife.

Those years taught me, long before the data boom, how profoundly a small device could transform daily life.

Then, in 2003, a quiet policy decision changed everything. Incoming calls were made free.[1] Almost overnight, India's telecom market opened like floodgates. Mobile penetration soared from negligible levels to over 100 million users within a few short years.[2]

For the first time, the same technology sat in the hands of both the wealthy and the working class. Geography no longer dictated access. A single device cut across income levels, professions, languages, and locations. What had begun as a luxury became India's first true mass digital instrument. The mobile phone stopped being a communication tool. It became, in many ways, the operating system for India's digital future.

---

[1]TRAI Notification on Calling Party Pays Regime, 2003.
[2]COAI Mobility Reports, 2003–2007.

The Rise of India's IT Engine

While consumers were discovering choice, India's IT services industry was shaping something far more foundational: the country's digital capability. Through the late 1990s and early 2000s, companies such as Infosys, TCS, Wipro, and HCL Technologies did far more than write code. They pioneered the Global Delivery Model, a method of building and running technology systems from India with a level of precision, cost-efficiency and process rigour the world had never seen before. This model scaled at a breathtaking pace, proving that India could not only participate in global markets but also lead them through intellectual rigour, operational discipline, and engineering excellence.

As these firms expanded, they built a vast pool(s) of digital talent. Young engineers became fluent in global standards. Process designers and enterprise architects learned to structure complex systems for Fortune 500 clients. Project managers mastered the coordination of teams across continents. Leaders emerged who understood scale, quality, and operational excellence. This was not just workforce development but a quiet, national capability-building exercise that transformed the country's economic psyche. For the first time in modern history, an entire generation saw itself not as participants in a developing economy but as contributors to the world's technology transformation.

I experienced this shift firsthand. In 2002, I joined Infosys as a faculty member at the Infosys Leadership Institute. Within those walls, I saw how scale could be transformative, not as a concept but as a living, breathing force. Thousands of young professionals arrived at the Mysore campus each week, trained rigorously, and were deployed across the globe.

The sheer ambition of the operation was humbling. It changed how people thought about themselves, their families, and their futures. It changed how India thought about its place in the world. For many of us, it felt as though a country that had long been defined by scarcity had suddenly discovered an abundance of talent, opportunity, and possibility.

By the mid-2000s, these threads had begun to converge. By 2005, India possessed something unusual for a developing nation: a population hungry for change, a device that connected them, and a workforce ready to build at a global scale. Much of the talent shaped in the IT services era would inspire the systems that defined India's digital future—from identity platforms to payment rails and startup ecosystems. What the country still lacked was the final ingredient: a national digital infrastructure that could bind these forces together and a governance guardrail that would sustain it. This came up next.

2

Emergence of the Digital State

Between 2006 and 2016, something unprecedented happened: India reinvented itself as a builder of digital public goods.

This was neither the Chinese model of state-owned platforms nor the American model of private monopolies. India arguably created one of the world's most distinctive models of open digital rails on which innovators could build.

This shift produced three foundational layers that reshaped the country's digital potential.

Aadhaar: The Identity Breakthrough

Before India could dream of becoming a digital economy, it needed a single, universal identity that was reliable, real-time and trusted across institutions. For decades, that did not exist. Identity was scattered across ration cards, voter IDs, birth certificates, and handwritten local documents: a patchwork that excluded millions, slowed down services, and created friction at every step. Aadhaar changed this by giving every resident a unique, verifiable identity, thereby unifying a fragmented system and making trust portable throughout the country.

Yet Aadhaar's true significance goes far beyond its billion-plus enrolments. It redefined how India delivers public services. Subsidies that once leaked through layers of intermediaries now move directly into bank accounts. Welfare schemes verify beneficiaries in seconds. Authentication that once depended on signatures, stamps and counters now takes seconds. In reducing friction, Aadhaar lowered the cost of inclusion, shrank the distance between citizen and state and made governance possible at a scale and speed unimaginable in the paper era.

Every system that came after—e-KYC, e-Sign, DigiLocker, UPI, FASTag and the Account Aggregator framework—rests on this ability to confirm identity instantly and reliably.

Much of this transformation owes its momentum to Nandan Nilekani, co-founder of Infosys. He led the Aadhaar mission with clarity of vision and a belief in India's potential. His contribution is not simply technological; it is civilizational. Millions who were once excluded from formal systems can now participate in the economy because Aadhaar made identity simple, respectful, and universal.

On a personal note, I feel privileged to have seen aspects of this leadership up close during my time at the Infosys Leadership Institute. Conducting strategy workshops with Mr Nilekani left a lasting impression, not because of his stature but because of his ability to combine bold technological thinking with a deep commitment to national impact. Those early interactions illuminated what Aadhaar would eventually become: not just a digital ID but a cornerstone of India's economic future.

Aadhaar did not merely solve a technical problem. It solved the identity problem for a billion people. In doing so, it unlocked the foundation of a digital nation.

While Aadhaar has attracted legitimate debate around privacy, exclusion and governance safeguards, few dispute its transformative effect on identity verification at scale.

India Stack: Building the Rails of Digital Life

If Aadhaar established identity, India Stack built the architecture on which that identity could be used. Few nations have attempted to create an open, interoperable set of digital rails that anyone could plug into, from governments and banks to fintech founders and neighbourhood kirana stores. India Stack turned the country's diversity and complexity from a logistical challenge into a technological opportunity.

At its core, India Stack allows people to prove who they are, sign what they need to, access the documents required and move money instantly. All this is done through digital protocols that work uniformly across the country. What appears simple on the surface took years of foundational design thinking. Each layer—e-KYC, e-Sign, DigiLocker, UPI, the Unified Health Interface and the Account Aggregator framework—removed a friction point that Indians had quietly lived with for decades.

Its genius lies in how various components work together. Identity verifies the person. Consent ensures control. Documentation provides proof. Payments complete the transaction. In India, this sequence once took days or weeks. With India Stack, it takes seconds.

Today, this infrastructure is so deeply embedded in everyday life that it is almost invisible. India Stack is omnipresent when:

- you can open a bank account only with your mobile phone in minutes.
- your PAN can be retrieved from DigiLocker.
- you can file your taxes without paperwork.
- you make the FASTag payment in two seconds.
- your doctor accesses your medical records with your one-time consent.

- a small merchant in a tier-3 town accepts UPI payments without a point-of-sale (POS) machine.

Your credit score, bank statements, and investment data move securely across institutions through an Account Aggregator because you allowed it.

These conveniences feel natural, but they are the result of one of the most quietly transformative digital architectures ever built.

India Stack also changed the economics of innovation. Previously, building a digital product in India meant navigating weeks of verification, paperwork, and compliance hurdles. Today, a startup can launch a financial app within a few days because KYC, payments, consent, and data-sharing are all standardized and ready to integrate. A small fintech innovator in Jaipur or Kochi has access to the same national infrastructure as the country's largest banks. This levelling of the playing field has been one of India Stack's most profound contributions.

It also transformed state capacity. Direct Benefit Transfers now reach millions with minimal leakage. Scholarships, pensions, LPG subsidies, and welfare payments land directly into Aadhaar-linked accounts. Government services no longer depend on files, stamps, and faxed documents because citizens authenticate with a fingerprint, sign with a digital certificate and receive online approvals.

In 2025, India Stack has normalized digital life. We rarely think about the protocol behind a QR payment or the trust layer behind a KYC authentication. Yet behind that ease lies a system that has reimagined how a nation of a billion people can transact, trust, and participate.

JAM: Inclusion at Scale

For decades, financial inclusion in India was an aspiration that struggled against structural realities. Bank branches were scarce in rural areas. Documentation requirements were cumbersome, and millions remained outside the formal financial system. The government had launched inclusion drives before, such as the nationalization of banks in 1969, the Lead Bank Scheme, and no-frills accounts in the 2000s.[3] These efforts, while well-intentioned, were limited by the constraints of a paper-driven economy. Access depended on geography. Verification depended on documents. Participation depended on physical presence.

Jan Dhan, Aadhaar and Mobile (JAM) changed that equation entirely.

The Jan Dhan Yojana, launched in 2014, resulted in the opening of bank accounts at an unprecedented scale. Aadhaar enabled instant identity verification. Mobile phones connected individuals to the financial system, regardless of their location. Together, they formed a digital spine that allowed the Government of India to deliver services, benefits and entitlements directly to citizens with reduced friction, leakage, or delay.

This convergence was the result of a clear vision by the Government of India to enable inclusion through infrastructure, not intermediaries. JAM enabled a shift from supply-led banking, where banks tried to reach citizens, to demand-led participation, where citizens could connect to the system on their own terms.

The outcome was transformative.

A farmer in Bihar, a domestic worker in Jaipur, and a

---

[3]Bank Nationalization 1969: RBI's History of Banking in India; Lead Bank Scheme 1969: RBI Lead Bank Scheme, RBI Guidelines and Reports; No Frills Accounts (2005 and onwards): Financial Inclusion by Extension of Banking Services—Use of 'No-Frills' Accounts.

fisherman in Tamil Nadu suddenly had equal access to formal savings, credit, insurance, and government benefits. A bank account became more than a place to store money. It became a channel for empowerment. Transparent, Aadhaar-linked Direct Benefit Transfers ensured subsidies reached intended beneficiaries, reducing leakage and saving the exchequer billions of rupees. These savings, in turn, allowed investment in infrastructure, welfare, and growth.

JAM's impact extends beyond governance. It affects the macro-economy. When millions join the financial system:

- savings increase,
- consumption becomes more predictable,
- credit markets deepen,
- insurance adoption rises,
- small businesses gain access to working capital, and
- household financial resilience improves.

Each of these contributes to higher productivity and long-term GDP growth.

Most importantly, JAM redefined inclusion itself. It was no longer about opening a bank account, but about ensuring that every citizen can participate in the economy, transact with dignity, access government services and build a more secure financial future. Inclusion stopped being a policy challenge and became a design accomplishment rooted in technology, identity, and connectivity.

JAM extended and redrew the boundaries of the formal economy. In doing so, it laid the economic foundation for a more confident and connected nation.

From State Capability to Market Transformation

The combined effect of Aadhaar, India Stack and JAM was not limited to governance. It fundamentally rewired the ecosystem in which Indian businesses operated. For the first time, companies could avail of universal identity, instant verification, seamless documentation, and real-time payments as default conditions. The cost of acquiring customers, authenticating transactions, and delivering benefits fell dramatically.

India's unit economics, long held back by distance, paperwork, and manual processes, was quietly being rewritten. A market that had once been too expensive to serve, too fragmented to organize and too slow to scale was suddenly primed for digital acceleration. All it needed was abundant, affordable data to ignite the system. When Jio triggered the data explosion of 2016, it didn't create a revolution—it released one that had already been engineered. With that final barrier removed, India became fertile ground for platforms to rise at unprecedented speed.

3

When Data Changed Everything

By 2016, India had the identity rails, digital architecture and financial systems, but the nation still awaited one final input: cheap, abundant data. When Jio entered the market, it delivered exactly that and at a scale that upended the economics of digital consumption overnight. Data prices fell dramatically, dropping by over 90 per cent,[4] and smartphones became as commonplace as feature phones had been just a few years earlier. India didn't ease into the digital world; it catapulted into it.

Within two years, the country became the world's largest consumer of mobile data,[5] driven not by a niche urban demographic but by a billion-strong population suddenly empowered to stream video, transact online and participate in the emerging digital economy. Jio unleashed what Aadhaar, India Stack and JAM had prepared. Digital behaviour, once premium, optional and uneven, became universal, habitual and instantaneous.

A Sudden Shift in Behaviour

The impact of this data explosion was not gradual—it was instantaneous. As soon as data became abundant, India's digital behaviour shifted almost overnight. Video consumption didn't

---

[4]Ericsson Mobility Report, 2018

[5]TRAI 'Telecom Indicators', 2018.

rise steadily; it surged. Families that once gathered around a single television now stream personalized content on individual screens. Payments that had relied on cash for generations migrated almost effortlessly to UPI, as if the country had been waiting for precisely this moment. Small merchants, many of whom had never used a POS machine, began accepting QR code payments within days. Social communication leapt from SMS and missed calls to WhatsApp, Instagram and short-form video platforms. Entire industries pivoted because consumers had already moved.

What made this moment extraordinary was not just the adoption, but the speed at which it became embedded in everyday life. Behaviours that typically evolve over decades in most societies were unfolded in India in a matter of months. A billion people simultaneously discovered a faster, cheaper and more convenient way of living, and once they experienced it, there was no going back.

4

The Emergence of the Platform Economy

By the late 2010s, India had assembled something rare: identity rails were in place, public digital infrastructure had matured, connectivity was widespread, financial inclusion had expanded and consumer behaviour was shifting at a pace rarely seen in any large democracy. It was only a matter of time before a new kind of business model took centre stage—not one built on assets or inventories but on interactions.

Platforms stepped into this environment with a force that felt almost preordained.

Unlike traditional businesses, platforms do not scale by adding factories, stores, or branches. They grow by expanding connections between buyers and sellers, riders and drivers, viewers and creators, and borrowers and lenders. Each additional user increases the value of the platform for others, creating a built-in advantage that compounds over time.

India, with its diversity, density, and digital fluency, became the perfect setting for this model to explode.

Why Platforms Scale So Powerfully

Platforms derive their power from a simple but profound idea: they become smarter with every interaction. Traditional businesses grow linearly with an extra store, branch, employee, etc. Platforms, by contrast, scale exponentially because each new user improves the experience for all existing users. A food delivery app that adds one restaurant increases choice for millions. A mobility platform that adds drivers reduces wait times across entire cities. A streaming service that studies viewer behaviour refines its recommendations, making the experience more engaging over time.

This is the logic of network effects, a system wherein scale improves quality rather than diluting it.

Platforms also automate trust. In the physical world, trust was built through familiarity—your neighbourhood shopkeeper, preferred travel agent or favourite taxi stand. Platforms translated that trust into ratings, reviews, algorithms, and digital assurances, enabling strangers to transact with confidence.

Their ability to lock in customers does not come from contracts or loyalty programmes but from the silent choreography of convenience: one-click payments, personalized feeds, instant discovery, and seamless fulfilment. Once consumers experience this level of efficiency, they rarely go back to the friction of the old world.

In India, where consumers eagerly embrace value and convenience, the platform model didn't just work, it thrived.

India's Platform Explosion

Once the foundations aligned, India witnessed one of the fastest large-scale platform expansions, with UPI rapidly coming to dominate over 80 per cent of retail digital payments.[6]

Entire industries began to reorganize themselves around digital intermediaries because consumers had already moved their attention and trust to apps.

---

[6]Copestake, Alexander, Divya Kirti, and Maria Soledad Martinez Peria, 'Growing Retail Digital Payments: The Value of Interoperability', International Monetary Fund, 25 June 2025, https://bit.ly/3S9vVBJ. Accessed on 29 May 2026.

Commerce moved from shelves to search bars.

Mobility shifted from taxi stands to algorithmic matching.

Food ordering evolved from printed menus to delivery dashboards.

Entertainment moved from linear broadcasts to personalized streaming.

Travel planning shifted from brochures and agents to real-time, app-based journeys.

Payments transitioned from cash, wallets and cards to UPI-based systems operating at near-zero cost.

Credit began moving from paper-based assessments to digital underwriting and Account Aggregator frameworks.

Platforms did not merely disrupt incumbents—they rewrote the logic of entire value chains. They changed where demand originates, how prices are determined, how trust is established, how services are delivered and who captures value.

For millions of Indians, platforms became the de facto gateway to daily life.

The question was no longer 'Where can I buy this?' but 'Which platform can get this to me fastest?'

This subtle shift in consumer psychology transformed the nature of competition across industries.

India's platform economy did not emerge gradually. It surged into existence because the infrastructure, consumer behaviour and incentives aligned with mathematical precision.

5

The Shift No One Saw Coming

Long before Indian incumbents realized what was happening, the customer had already crossed over to a different world. Discovery had shifted from aisles to apps. Persuasion had moved from advertising to algorithmic recommendations. Payments had migrated from cash to UPI. Loyalty had moved from brands to platforms.

At first, these seemed like small, almost incidental changes, even though rapid in nature—one QR code here, one online order there. But together, they formed a pattern: the centre of gravity in the value chain was shifting away from producers and towards platforms. The platform, not the brand, was becoming the first point of customer interaction. The platform, not the distributor, owned the relationship. The platform, not the retailer, shaped consumer behaviour. The nature of demand aggregation had fundamentally changed.

Incumbents saw the sales numbers, the rise of online traffic and customers comparing prices before entering stores, but they missed the deeper narrative.

Their customers hadn't left them for a better competitor. They had moved to an entirely new system.

This was the quiet beginning of disruption. The market had moved. The consumer had moved. But leadership mindsets had not.

The Fault Lines Beneath the Surface

What unfolded over the next few years was not random disruption, but the surfacing of deeper fault lines—pressures that had been building beneath the surface of Indian business for some time.

India's platform era introduced three fault lines that determine how incumbents respond to disruption:

- Format Obsolescence
- Platform Displacement
- Governance Gaps

Each of these will be explored in depth in Part II and through the case studies that follow.

Why This Chapter Matters

If the earlier chapters explained the first shift, tracing India's journey from a controlled economy to a liberalized one, and then from liberalization to a digitally-enabled society, this chapter marks the second shift—from a digital economy to a platform-driven one. Understanding this transition is essential to make sense of the following:

- Why did some giants collapse?
- Why were some displaced?
- Why were some disintermediated?
- Why did others reinvent themselves?

We now decode the three fault lines and bring them to life through the journeys of companies such as Moser Baer, Zee, MTV, HMT, Jet Airways, BSNL and others.

Part Two

THE THREE FAULT LINES OF PLATFORM DISRUPTION

6

Why Businesses Fail the Platform World

India's transition into a platform economy did not happen gently. It unfolded through rapid format shifts and technology-driven realignments that caught incumbents off guard. Executives saw demand grow, digital adoption rise and new consumer behaviours emerge, yet they underestimated how quickly platforms could tilt an entire industry.

This chapter explains why so many legacy companies failed to adapt, despite having resources, talent, and brand equity.

Before we turn to the case studies, it's useful to pause and clarify two basic concepts central to this discussion that distinguishes a platform business from a traditional one, and what exactly we mean by a 'fault line'.

Platform Business vs. a Pipeline Business

Most incumbents in India were built as pipeline businesses with linear value chains, whereby companies produce, distribute, and sell goods or services. Value flows in one direction, and advantage comes from owning and controlling assets like inventory, branches, fleets, stores, and physical distribution networks. For example, Retailers traditionally bought and stocked goods and sold them across their counters. Banks expanded through branches to reach depositors and borrowers. Taxi companies managed fleets and drivers to run tightly controlled operations.

Platforms invert this logic entirely. Instead of pushing products through a linear chain, they enable interactions. A retail platform doesn't sell what it owns. Instead, it connects millions of buyers and sellers, redefining discovery and choice. A financial platform doesn't rely on physical branches. It uses UPI, wallets and digital credit marketplaces to rewire how consumers initiate and complete financial transactions. Mobility platforms don't own vehicles; they match supply and demand in real time, using data, trust systems and algorithms to coordinate the system.

When a platform enters a sector, it doesn't simply add a new channel, it changes how discovery works, how trust is built, how pricing is set, and where value migrates. This foundational shift is the backdrop against which India's three fault lines must be understood.

What Are Fault Lines?

Fault lines are not obvious infirmities. They are structural vulnerabilities that become visible only when digital platforms enter a sector. Leaders rarely see them early because they are not apparent in annual plans, quarterly reviews, or P&Ls. Instead, they lie beneath the organization's operating logic

Platforms expose these fault lines through shifts in the following:

i. Consumption behaviour
ii. Discovery and demand aggregation
iii. Value migration and capture
iv. Organizational decision-making speed

Across industries, the same three fault lines have consistently predicted which companies adapt, which reinvent themselves and which ones collapse.

Fault Line One: Format Obsolescence

When the format dies, the business dies.

Format obsolescence occurs when the fundamental format, through which consumers access value, changes and renders the legacy format irrelevant. This is not a competition among firms. It is the retirement of an entire mode of consumption.

Across India, entire formats were attacked overnight. Some vanished completely, while others had to deal with significant damage. Cable TV gave way to OTT streaming, and DVDs were replaced by on-demand digital platforms. Physical retail ceded ground to e-commerce and hyperlocal delivery, though some physical retailers like Reliance Retail, D-Mart, etc., have adapted. Branch-led banking is being increasingly challenged by mobile-first interfaces. However, top-tier Indian banks, both private and public, are responding admirably.

These were format shifts that permanently rewired consumer behaviour.

The disruption is unforgiving because of the following:

- Consumers don't shift to a better competitor. They shift to a new format.
- Operational excellence cannot save a dying format.
- Decline often appears gradual at first, then becomes irreversible.

Executives often misinterpret format shifts as temporary dips, discounting cycles, or youth-driven trends, but they are irreversible.

a) Vodafone Idea didn't lose to Jio only on price. It lost to a new format of abundant, always-on data.
b) Retailers didn't lose to Amazon. They lost to a new

format of discovery and the network effects of a dominant platform.

While Format Obsolescence is potentially brutal, it does not always eliminate the old format; it can also reduce it to a niche. The critical question is whether the dominant mode of consumption changes.

Fault Line Two: Platform Displacement and Disintermediation

Even when the format remains intact, businesses can lose their direct relationship with the customer. Platform displacement happens when customer discovery, access and decision-making shift from brands to aggregators.

In India's platform era, consumers don't begin with brands. They begin with a platform whether Amazon, Google, Zomato, YouTube, Flipkart, Ola, Swiggy, MakeMyTrip, PhonePe, Instagram, Meesho and others.

In this shift, while platforms become the gateway, brands become suppliers. Demand aggregation is controlled by the platforms as brands get commoditized and lose relevance.

This has severe implications:

- Platforms own behavioural data, while brands lose consumer insight.
- Platforms control price visibility, leading to margin erosion for the brands.
- Algorithms determine visibility, and brands lose bargaining power.
- Platforms own the customer journey, and the brands lose loyalty.

Displacement typically evolves into disintermediation, whereby platforms start offering value directly.

Disintermediation does not mean that incumbents disappear

overnight. More often, they continue to perform important functions while steadily losing influence over the customer relationship. Banks still hold deposits. Hotels still provide rooms. Studios still create content. But the platform increasingly determines discovery, access, loyalty, and economics. The intermediary remains in the system, yet becomes progressively less central to how value is experienced and captured.

Many incumbents saw rising revenues and misread that as success, unaware that platforms were quietly capturing customer mindshare.

Fault Line Three: Governance Gaps

This refers to the inability to reallocate attention, resources, and authority despite recognizing environmental shifts.

Governance gaps arise when organizations recognize environmental shifts but fail to reallocate attention, resources, incentives, and decision rights quickly enough to respond. The issue is rarely an absence of capability. More often, it reflects structural inertia embedded in governance systems, capital allocation processes, organizational incentives and decision-making architectures.

In many cases, incumbents do not lose because they fail to recognize disruption. They lose because their governance systems are unable to translate recognition into timely action.

Signs of a Governance Gap

- The organization repeatedly pilots but rarely scales.
- Digital initiatives sit outside the core business.
- Resource allocation favours legacy revenue pools.
- Leaders acknowledge disruption publicly but delay strategic commitments.

The fault lines are analytical lenses rather than mutually exclusive categories. Most disruptions involve more than one fault line, although one usually dominates.

Building Leadership Foresight

By understanding these fault lines, leaders can detect disruption before it causes irreparable financial damage. They function as early-warning signals that reveal where value is migrating, why control is shifting, and how quickly the ground beneath an industry is moving.

Sudden shifts in consumption patterns signal that consumer habits are migrating to a new format, an early indicator of format obsolescence. Leaders must ask: Is my industry's underlying consumption model or customer behaviour changing faster than my business can adapt?

When customers begin discovering products through aggregators rather than brands, it reflects a redistribution of demand and influence, an unmistakable sign of platform displacement. The essential question becomes: am I still the starting point of the customer journey, or have I already been pushed downstream?

When platforms start offering the same value directly, bypassing traditional intermediaries, it marks the onset of platform disintermediation, where incumbents progressively lose relevance. Leaders must confront the harder question: is the platform preparing to take over parts of my value chain that I once owned?

When leadership hesitates, debates, or delays decisions, it exposes internal misalignment, an early manifestation of a governance gap. leaders must ask: is my organization structurally capable of confronting and responding to the risks platforms introduce?

With this foresight, leaders can anticipate which industries are likely to be disrupted next, recognize which business models are becoming structurally fragile, understand where value is poised to migrate and identify the organizational shifts required to stay competitive in a platform-driven economy.

Now that the fault lines are established, the natural question is how they manifest in the real world?

Patterns that seem abstract at a conceptual level become evident when viewed through actual market shifts and strategic responses. The case studies that follow depict these fault lines. Rather than presenting them as post-mortems, these cases help leaders recognize the early signals they may have missed, strategic pivots they could have made sooner, and subtle ways in which value migration unfolds. Taken together, they offer hindsight and a practical lens through which leaders can interpret change in their own sectors calmly, clearly, and ahead of time.

7

When the Format Disappeared: The Fall of Moser Baer

The first case we will discuss is that of Moser Baer, which is one of the clearest examples of format obsolescence in India's technology landscape.

For years, the company dominated the global market for CDs and DVDs in an era when value was accessed through physical media, optical drives and home libraries. As digital formats rose, consumer behaviour shifted rapidly towards MP3s, downloads and, eventually, streaming.

The environment was displaying unmistakable signs of value migration. Devices began to drop disc drives. Broadband penetration increased. Global entertainment consumption was moving online. Yet Moser Baer doubled down on its pipeline strength in terms of manufacturing scale, low-cost production, and physical distribution with the belief that the format would endure.

The result was a classic format-collapse scenario. Even a world-class incumbent with scale, brand trust, and operational excellence could not survive a future where the format through which customers accessed value no longer existed.

The World of Global Optical Media before the Fall

To understand the scale of what followed, it is necessary to return to the world that existed before the decline began.

In the early 2000s, optical media was woven into everyday life. Across India, street vendors sold stacks of CDs and DVDs. Personal computers were loaded with software through discs, from operating systems to antivirus programmes. Homes displayed collections of films, music albums, and games. Offices backed up data on rewritable CDs, while students carried project files on recordable DVDs. A new computer was expected to include an optical drive. Digital value, for most consumers, still arrived in physical form.

Globally, this translated into a large and profitable industry. By the middle of the decade, optical media had become a multi-billion-dollar business, producing tens of billions of discs annually. Optical drives were standard in most personal computers, reflecting the extent to which the format had penetrated homes, schools, and workplaces. Production was concentrated in Asian manufacturing hubs such as Taiwan, China, Malaysia, and India. The business demanded scale, precision engineering, and licensing capability, which created meaningful barriers to entry.

The economics of the sector were distinctive. Success depended on high asset utilization, operational efficiency, and large-volume orders. A significant share of revenues came from OEM relationships and export markets, linking manufacturers to distributors and brand owners in Japan, Europe, and the United States. These channels, in turn, supplied retailers and entertainment networks worldwide. Music labels, film studios, and software companies still relied heavily on physical formats to reach mass audiences.

Even the informal economy revolved around discs. Unauthorized copying, street distribution, and local resale networks were largely physical businesses built around CDs and DVDs.

It was in this environment that Moser Baer India Limited

emerged as a global force. At its peak, the company ranked among the world's largest optical media producers, exported to more than eighty countries and operated at efficiencies comparable to leading manufacturers in Taiwan and China. It was not merely participating in the industry; it was one of the companies helping define it.

Yet beneath the scale and confidence of the era lay a vulnerability that many incumbents underestimated. The industry depended on a technology model whose durability would soon be tested.

Early Warning Signs

The decline did not begin with a dramatic collapse. It started with signals that were easy to dismiss while DVD demand remained healthy and shipments still ran into the billions.

One of the clearest signals came from device design. In 2008, Apple Inc. launched the MacBook Air without a built-in optical drive, prioritizing thinness and portability over legacy hardware. That same year, global notebook shipments edged past desktop shipments for the first time. Mobility was beginning to matter more than expansion slots and disc trays.

By 2010, portable PCs had become the largest segment of the global computer market. Laptops were no longer a premium niche; they were becoming the default choice for many consumers. As that shift gathered pace, optical drives moved from a standard feature to optional extra across much of the notebook category.

At the same time, digital access patterns were changing. Music downloads expanded rapidly, broadband penetration improved and online piracy became easier to scale. In urban India, younger users were already shifting away from shelves of discs towards files stored on hard drives and content obtained online. Ownership was starting to give way to access.

Individually, these developments appeared manageable. Collectively, they pointed to something more serious: the infrastructure supporting physical media was beginning to weaken.

Many incumbents failed to respond because the legacy business still looked healthy. Revenues had not yet collapsed, customers still existed and factories were still running. Established organizations are often guided by familiar metrics, and early shifts rarely appear dangerous when measured against the success patterns of the previous decade.

When the Shift Became Irreversible (2010–2020)

If the earlier period revealed warning signs, the following decade made the outcome unmistakable.

The most visible change occurred in the PC ecosystem. Optical drives, once standard in personal computers, began disappearing from new devices, especially laptops. Manufacturers preferred slimmer designs, lighter machines, and larger batteries. What had once been built into nearly every computer increasingly became an external accessory for those who still needed it.

Software distribution evolved just as quickly. Applications and operating systems that had once arrived on CDs or DVDs were increasingly delivered through downloads, app stores and USB installation media. Consumers who once stored software, music, and films on shelves found that much of the same content could now be accessed instantly or stored in the cloud.

Demand for physical entertainment formats also contracted sharply. DVD revenues declined across major markets, while global CD sales fell steeply from their earlier peak. Streaming platforms, digital rentals, and subscription services changed consumer behaviour by making convenience more attractive than ownership. Physical media did not disappear overnight, but it moved steadily from mainstream product to specialist niche.

Once volumes began to fall, the economics of the industry deteriorated quickly. Factories designed for enormous output depended on scale, predictable utilization, and efficient logistics. As demand weakened, those advantages eroded. High fixed-cost businesses that had thrived in an era of mass consumption found themselves exposed in a market that no longer needed their core product.

What changed the industry was not a single competitor or one breakthrough technology. It was the cumulative force of several data-driven shifts—faster networks, better devices, cloud distribution, and changing consumer habits. By the time the decline became obvious, the foundations had already moved.

The Rise of Streaming

As physical media receded, the rise of streaming created a parallel digital universe that was faster, cheaper, and more convenient. This shift unfolded across four reinforcing layers.

First, connectivity improved dramatically. According to Akamai's historical reports, global average internet speeds rose several-fold during the decade, while peak speeds increased even faster.[7] As bandwidth expanded and reliability improved, streaming became progressively easier and more mainstream.

India experienced an even sharper shift. Intense telecom competition in the second half of the decade pushed mobile data

---

[7]'Global Average Internet Connection Speed Increases 26% Year Over Year, Akamai Reports » TechWorm', *TechBloat*, 28 January 2025, https://bit.ly/3RGaKXS. Accessed on 29 May 2026.

prices sharply lower, making internet access affordable to mass consumers. Streaming moved quickly from a premium activity to an everyday habit.

Second, the device changed. India's transition to mobile-first entertainment was swift. By the end of the 2010s, India had nearly 500 million smartphone users, making it one of the world's largest handset markets.[8]

Video consumption followed the handset. By the late 2010s, India had become one of YouTube's largest and fastest-growing markets, powered primarily by mobile viewing. The screen that mattered most for digital entertainment was no longer the television or the desktop computer. It was the smartphone in the user's hand.

Taken together, faster connectivity and mobile access reduced the relevance of discs, players and physical distribution networks, replacing them with on-demand access delivered through apps and cloud platforms.

Third, business models evolved. Streaming platforms scaled globally and in India within a few years:

- Netflix passed 100 million global streaming users by 2017.
- Hotstar became India's largest OTT platform by 2018.
- Amazon Prime Video crossed 10 million Indian users by 2018.

Subscription pricing, on-demand access, and personalized recommendations appealed to consumers in ways physical formats never could. Streaming wasn't just a new distribution method but a new behavioural norm.

---

[8]Mishra, Deepak, et al., 'State of India's Digital Economy', IPCIDE, February 2023, https://bit.ly/4vdANVj. Accessed on 30 May 2026.

Finally, emerging markets like India did not transition gradually, they leapfrogged. With less than 10 per cent of Indian households owning DVD players in 2010, the shift to digital bypassed physical formats entirely. Smartphone access grew 10 to 20 times faster than DVD-player adoption. The markets that incumbents expected to grow into simply never arrived.

The supply-side economics of content delivery also transformed.

Physical media required heavy investment—manufacturing plants, machinery, inventory, and distribution networks. Each unit carried a cost.

Streaming, by contrast, was software-driven. Content could be distributed through cloud infrastructure, scaled instantly, and delivered at near-zero marginal cost.

In one model, growth demanded more machines, more floorspace, and more working capital. In the other, scale came with minimal friction. The future was digital and defined by software.

This was not simply a change in format. It was a complete redefinition of how value was created and delivered.

Even when the data is compelling, disruption rarely appears as a single, decisive trend. Instead, it shows up as a series of subtle shifts, each easy to explain in isolation but transformative in combination. Incumbent organization are built to track volumes, margins and market share, not the early behaviours that emerge outside the core. When a company has decades of success behind it, existing mental models become the strongest lens through which new information is interpreted. It's not denial or overconfidence but the natural tendency of organizations to trust the datasets that have historically served them well, even when the real story lies in the weak signals at the edges. This is the context in which Moser Baer's strategic choices must be understood.

Moser Baer's Strategic Missteps

Moser Baer's strategy in the late 2000s reflected a deep confidence in the continuity of the optical media business. From its vantage point, the logic was sound. Global DVD demand still ran into billions of units, and the company's manufacturing advantage appeared both durable and scalable. Each strategic decision therefore made sense within the framework of the pipeline era. However, these decisions steered the company further away from the emerging digital reality.

Even as early digital signals began to surface, Moser Baer continued to expand aggressively between 2006 and 2009. The report states that depreciation rose 27 per cent because of capacity expansion in optical media and entertainment businesses.[9]

It invested heavily in new production lines and increased capacity positioning itself for what it believed would be sustained global volume growth. Annual reports from the period reflected confidence and strong capex commitments. In hindsight, these investments locked the company deeper into a capital-intensive model at a time when the world was preparing to move away from physical media.

In 2007, Moser Baer acquired a controlling stake in OM&T BV, Philips' Netherlands-based optical media technology and R&D subsidiary.[10] The deal was intended to strengthen Moser Baer's innovation capabilities, particularly in next-generation formats such as Blu-ray, and to reinforce its technological edge in global optical media. Yet, as digital consumption accelerated, the strategic value of optical R&D began to diminish. What had once been an

---

[9]'Moser Baer India Ltd.: Q4 FY 2008 Update', *Business Standard*, 2 May 2008, https://bit.ly/4uGeMOI. Accessed on 29 May 2026.

[10]'Moser Baer Buys 81% Stake in Philips Optical Media R&D Unit', *The Economic Times*, 7 February 2007, https://bit.ly/3Qccxn4. Accessed on 29 May 2026.

important competitive asset became progressively less relevant—not because the technology lacked merit, but because the format it served was steadily losing commercial and cultural relevance.

A similar misread emerged with Blu-ray. The company believed that Blu-ray represented the next big format at a moment when the world was moving away from discs altogether. By 2014, Blu-ray's growth curve had begun to flatten just as streaming moved decisively into the mainstream. Physical media revenues came under increasing pressure, and although falling hardware prices had made entry-level Blu-ray players broadly affordable by 2012, lower device costs were not enough to halt the long-term consumer shift towards on-demand digital consumption.

As optical media faced disruption, Moser Baer redirected significant capital into thin-film solar, planning 600 MW of capacity and attracting large orders.[11]

This move created a second capital-intensive vertical at a time when global solar dynamics were undergoing rapid disruption. Between 2009 and 2012, Chinese manufacturers flooded the market, making thin-film globally uncompetitive against crystalline technologies. Instead of pivoting towards digital distribution or new software-led models, Moser Baer doubled down on physical manufacturing, replicating the same structural exposure that was already hurting its core business. In effect, diversification reinforced the same constraints it intended to reduce.

Missing India's Digital Moment

While global streaming accelerated, India was undergoing its own digital revolution. The country was rapidly transitioning

---

[11]'Moser Baer Secures US $500M in Thin-film Module Orders', *Renewable Energy World*, 21 October 2008, https://bit.ly/4wX3Mhn. Accessed on 29 May 2026.

from 3G to 4G networks, with broadband subscribers rising from 136.53 million in December 2015 to 149.75 million in March 2016, according to the Telecom Regulatory Authority of India (TRAI), a growth of 9.69%.[12] Internet subscribers rose to 342.65 million by March 2016, up from 302.35 million a year earlier.

Smartphone adoption was also scaling quickly. By 2014–15, India had already crossed approximately 159 million mobile internet users, 119 million urban and 40 million rural, as per IAMAI reports.[13]

At the same time, OTT and digital video consumption surged as cheap mobile data and wider 4G access transformed viewing habits. TRAI's Wireless Data Services report shows that total mobile data usage exploded from 4,642 million GB in 2016 to 46,406 million GB in 2018—a nearly tenfold increase in two years, reflecting the rapid rise of streaming and app-based media consumption.[14]

Even then, Moser Baer continued scaling DVD production in a market that had never fully adopted DVDs in the first place. The company remained aligned with global demand patterns, even as the Indian consumer ecosystem leapfrogged physical formats entirely. This was a consequence of strategy being anchored in a world that no longer existed.

By the early 2010s, the forces reshaping the industry had begun to crystallize, with clear structural fault lines that steadily

[12]'The Indian Telecom Services Performance Indicators, January–March, 2016', TRAI, 5 August 2016, https://bit.ly/4eMo3y3. Accessed on 30 May 2026.

[13]'Internet in India 2014', IAMAI, 18 November 2014, https://bit.ly/4uV3q8V. Accessed on 30 May 2026.

[14]'Yearly Performance Indicators of Indian Telecom Sector (Second Edition), 2017', TRAI, 4 May 2018, https://bit.ly/4eba99z; 'Wireless Data Services in India: An Analytical Report', TRAI, 21 August 2019, https://bit.ly/4fLTSZM. Both accessed on 30 May 2026.

weakened Moser Baer's business model. Each fault line expressed itself differently, but together, they created a shift that no manufacturing-led strategy could absorb.

The first was format obsolescence. The most decisive change came from the complete transformation of how consumers accessed digital value. Streaming replaced ownership. Cloud storage displaced local backups. Mobile devices, rather than DVD players or PCs, became the primary screen. The disc was no longer necessary.

The second was platform displacement, as they began replacing traditional distribution channels. YouTube became India's largest video destination; Netflix, iTunes, and Hotstar became the gateways for global and local entertainment, and mobile apps replaced physical catalogues and shelves. The starting point of the customer journey had shifted.

The third was internal. Moser Baer's core strengths of manufacturing efficiency, scale, and process discipline were optimized for an era where physical formats mattered. As digital behaviour accelerated, capital remained tied to manufacturing assets, decisions followed traditional cycles, and the organization continued to bet on format evolution (Blu-ray, thin-film, and capacity expansions).

The Tipping Point

Between 2012 and 2017, the fault lines converged, the timelines for which are as follows:

- 2011–2012: Laptops had largely stopped supporting optical drives, effectively ending the hardware foundation of the DVD ecosystem.
- 2013: YouTube India's explosive growth made digital video mainstream.

- 2015–2016: India's 4G rollout and Hotstar's rapid scale profoundly reshaped access and viewing habits.
- 2016–2017: After Jio's entry, India became the world's cheapest mobile-data market, making streaming accessible to the mass market almost overnight.

The tipping point was not a moment of collapse but the culmination of a decade of signals. Once consumers began streaming high-quality videos on low-cost data networks through inexpensive smartphones, the logic of manufacturing billions of physical discs ceased to exist.

What Really Went Wrong

Moser Baer did not fail because of a single misstep but a structural collision between its business model and the three fault lines:

- Format obsolescence removed the need for the product.
- Platform displacement removed the channels through which demand once flowed.
- Governance gaps slowed the organization's ability to reposition itself before the shift became irreversible.

By the time the tipping point arrived, the format had vanished, platforms had captured the customer relationship, and the organization's capital was locked into a model the market no longer needed. The business did not fail because it executed poorly. It failed because the world changed faster than a manufacturing-led model could adapt.

Lessons for Leaders

The Moser Baer story offers several enduring lessons for leaders navigating today's platform economy. The first is that when a format disappears, no level of operational excellence can compensate.

Second, emerging markets do not always follow linear adoption curves. They often leapfrog.

Third, companies with capex-heavy models must track technological shifts with exceptional discipline because their commitments are long-term, whereas consumer behaviour can change overnight.

Fourth, leaders must distinguish format evolution from digital transformation: CD to DVD to Blu-ray was evolution, but streaming redefined the category altogether. Finally, sunk-cost governance is real. Organizations built on manufacturing strength often find it hardest to pivot to asset-light, software-led models. These lessons are not about looking back but about equipping leaders with the foresight to recognize similar patterns before their industries are reshaped.

Moser Baer's story is not unique. Across industries in India, similar patterns have played out: sometimes more gradually, sometimes more visibly, but driven by the same underlying forces.

The next case reveals how a different industry encountered the same fault lines—and how the outcome, while shaped by context, followed a strikingly familiar arc.

8

When the Interface Shifts: The Zee Story

This chapter relies on publicly available information, and I interpret strategic outcomes through the fault line framework. I do not seek to assess management intent, internal deliberations, or executive competence.

While Moser Baer showed us what happens when a format dies, Zee Entertainment reveals what happens when the interface shifts. The collapse of Moser Baer was abrupt and absolute because the physical medium—CDs and DVDs—became irrelevant.

Here, the underlying demand for video content did not disappear. In fact, it exploded. What collapsed instead was the strategic position of a once-dominant incumbent in the value chain. Zee is the archetypal case of platform displacement, a disruption not of content but of the platforms that control discovery, distribution, and customer relationships.

Platform displacement occurs when the centre of gravity in an industry shifts from the producer to the platform that aggregates, personalizes, and delivers experiences. In such markets, incumbents often continue doing what made them successful—creating strong content, optimizing operations, and managing channels—but they lose control over the customer interface, which progressively migrates to platforms powered by data, algorithms, and scale. When that happens, even well-run companies with deep domain experience find themselves competing in the wrong battlefield.

In the Zee case, we will see how India's first private broadcaster—an organization that thrived across multiple eras of media evolution—found itself increasingly displaced by global platforms, domestic aggregators, and emerging digital ecosystems. The underlying demand for content did not diminish; what shifted was control over discovery, engagement, and customer relationships. This narrative explores why content strength, while necessary, became insufficient in the absence of ownership of the data and interface layers through which audiences increasingly accessed media. It examines how discoverability engines rewrote the economics of attention and how legacy assumptions can prevent incumbents from recognizing such shifts in time. Above all, this case helps leaders understand the profound difference between owning content and owning the interface—and why, in a platform era, the latter increasingly determines who wins the customer.

Building India's First Private Broadcast Empire

When Zee entered the Indian media scene in 1992, it entered an industry characterized by scarcity and government control. Doordarshan dominated the airwaves. Content options were limited, and television was a rationed commodity, with viewers having access to only a handful of choices. In this highly regulated environment, Zee did something remarkable. It created India's first private broadcasting network.

Under Subhash Chandra's leadership, the company created a strategic plan that was simultaneously daring and perfectly suited for the time. It recognized the country's appetite for variety long before data or analytics could confirm it. It made a contrarian bet and invested in regional programming when others focused only on national content. It built distribution muscle through cable networks, understanding that reach would determine influence

And perhaps most importantly, Zee mastered the art of serialized storytelling that built daily viewing habits and deep household loyalty.

The success of this strategy is evident in its results: a wide portfolio of channels across genres and languages. By the mid-2000s, Zee had evolved into one of India's most influential integrated media groups, spanning entertainment, movies, news, regional broadcasting, distribution, and direct-to-home television because of the following:

a. a strong advertising-led revenue model,
b. a growing subscription base and
c. an integrated content-to-distribution pipeline.

For nearly 20 years, it thrived in a world where scarcity defined advantage. Limited bandwidth and high entry barriers meant that those who controlled distribution controlled attention. During this time, Zee did almost everything right: outperforming rivals, growing faster than international players, and becoming an integral part of Indian television culture.

At its peak, Zee was more than just a successful broadcaster; it was a case study in strategic clarity. Ironically, this very success and the mindset it created later made it difficult to recognize the next wave of platform-driven disruption.

When Scarcity Gave Way to Abundance

By the mid-2010s, the foundations of India's media industry began to shift. At first, the changes were gradual. Then they accelerated. What had long been a supply-constrained market was suddenly flooded with abundant, always-available digital access. Three forces combined to redraw the map:

- ultra-cheap mobile data
- rapid smartphone adoption
- affordable, high-quality 4G streaming
- a growing cultural appetite for on-demand, personalized viewing

The choke points that had protected incumbents, namely, satellite bandwidth, cable capacity, and prime-time slots, no longer mattered. Consumers no longer waited for content. Instead, content waited for them.

As distribution became abundant, the influence of traditional gatekeepers diminished. Power swiftly moved to platforms, systems that aggregated content, personalized discovery, and controlled the interface through which viewers engaged. The new centres of gravity were no longer broadcasters, but:

- streaming platforms with vast libraries,
- recommendation engines driven by data,
- global players with deep capital and technology, and
- device ecosystems that controlled access points.

In the new ecosystem, while content ownership remained important, but it was no longer sufficient on its own. What mattered was who controlled the interface, data layer, and behavioural signals that shaped viewer choice. Platforms, not broadcasters, became the new custodians of attention.

For Zee, a strategically savvy, deeply execution-driven incumbent, this shift was profoundly counterintuitive. Its entire business model had been shaped in an era where great content, distribution muscle, and brand familiarity guaranteed dominance. And paradoxically, even as the demand for content exploded, the way consumers accessed content had fundamentally changed. For a growing segment of viewers, loyalty increasingly shifted from channels to platforms that offered frictionless discovery, personalization, and abundant choice.

New actors in the value chain, such as telcos, device manufacturers, app ecosystems, and global aggregators, began exerting power that broadcasters had never faced before. The industry's centre of gravity moved from production to orchestration.

Zee, like many incumbents, believed its legacy moat would endure, but the moat was built for a world of scarcity. In a world of abundance, the platform, not the broadcaster, owned the viewer relationship, and that single shift transformed the competitive landscape forever.

Zee's Strategic Missteps in a Changing Market

To its credit, Zee sensed early that digital consumption would reshape India's media landscape. It moved quickly to launch Zee5, well before several domestic broadcasters had even defined a streaming roadmap. However, the real challenge in the OTT era was never about launching a digital product. It was about recognizing that the industry had entered a fundamentally new competitive paradigm governed by data moats, discovery engines, and interface ownership rather than by content volume alone.

Like many strong incumbents, Zee carried forward the mental models of a world it had dominated. These legacy assumptions, which were perfectly valid in the broadcast era, shaped how the organization framed digital disruption. Zee's missteps were not failures of intent or execution but of strategic reframing, classic patterns seen across industries when the basis of competition shifts.

Three such patterns defined its early digital trajectory.

Error 1: Extending the Old Model Instead of Building a New One

Zee's response suggests that OTT may initially have been framed as an extension of television rather than as a distinct platform business.

Three choices reflected this TV-first mindset:

- Content volume over data depth: Relative to several leading OTT platforms, Zee appeared slower in embedding data capabilities, recommendation systems, and behavioural analytics at the core of its digital model.
- TV and digital as parallel worlds: The separation between broadcast and digital operations may have limited opportunities to build unified audience intelligence.
- Programming logic over platform logic: Decision-making continued to be shaped by release calendars and scheduling rhythms rather than by user behaviour patterns, cohort analysis, or personalized discovery.

While global and domestic OTT leaders engineered behavioural flywheels—systems where data improves discovery and discovery drives engagement—Zee scaled content without scaling the data moat behind it.

This reflects one of the classic traps of digital transformation: incumbents often use technology to optimize the legacy model, while disruptors use it to reinvent the business itself.

Zee's early OTT strategy appears to have extended several assumptions of the broadcast era into the digital domain.

Error 2: Misreading the Competitive Battlefield

Zee was not alone in confronting the digital wave. Star, Sony, and Viacom18 also had to navigate the shift. What differentiated Zee was the persistence of its historical competitive frame.

For two decades, Zee had competed intensely with its broadcast peers for ratings, ad share, and distribution strength. Its strategic response suggests that the emerging OTT landscape may initially have been interpreted through the lens of traditional broadcast competition.

In Zee's worldview, the contest was still broadcaster-versus-broadcaster, but the real battlefield had already shifted.

But the real competitors were no longer traditional peers. They were platforms:

- YouTube, with its vast creator ecosystem,
- Amazon Prime Video, integrated into a broader digital ecosystem,
- Netflix, deploying global capital and data, and
- Hotstar, combining sports, entertainment, and technology at scale.

Increasingly, competition extended beyond broadcaster-versus-broadcaster dynamics to include platform-versus-platform economics.

How Zee's Rivals Responded

All broadcasters faced the same disruption, but their responses reflected different levels of platform awareness:

Star (later Disney Star)

Star made the earliest and boldest pivot. With Hotstar, it did the following:

- used sports (especially IPL) as a digital anchor.
- invested heavily in engineering and streaming infrastructure.
- embedded data and personalization into the core of the product.

Star reframed the competition: OTT is the new primary interface, not a digital extension of television.

Sony

Sony adopted a differentiated approach with SonyLIV:

- doubling down on crime, thrillers and distinct originals,
- building selective partnerships, and
- choosing depth over raw scale.

It was a smaller pivot in absolute terms but strategically aware of digital's different grammar.

Viacom18/Colors

Viacom18, supported by Reliance, built JioCinema into a mass-scale platform through the following:

- Jio's massive distribution base,
- aggressive acquisition of sports rights, and
- a low-friction, ecosystem-led mass model.

This was not just a strategy; it was an advantage built across networks, devices, and data.

Error 3: When the Gatekeepers Changed

The most disruptive shift came from players that did not create content at all but controlled how viewers accessed it. These new intermediaries, namely, telcos, device manufacturers, operating systems, and aggregators, quietly rewired power in the media value chain.

The new gatekeepers were as follows:

- Telcos bundling streaming services into data plans, shifting loyalty away from apps to telecom ecosystems.

- Smart TVs promoting platform apps and universal search over linear channels.
- Aggregators like Prime Video and Apple TV, which turned individual OTT apps into secondary destinations.
- YouTube, which captured extraordinary watch time through creator ecosystems and algorithmic discovery.

In this environment, control moved away from the creator. It moved to the interface. Zee found itself pushed one layer down the stack. It was still a respected content creator but no longer the viewer's default entry point. Underestimating new intermediaries is common across industries; challengers often emerge not as product competitors but as interface displacers.

Lessons for Leaders

Zee's journey illustrates a core principle of platform-era competition: dominance is rarely lost through operational decline. It is typically lost through strategic reframing that arrives too late. In the broadcast era, Zee built a formidable moat through content scale, strong distribution, and deep cultural resonance. The rise of digital platforms did not directly erode these strengths. Instead, it changed the basis on which value was created, shifting power from content ownership to interface ownership, from programming judgement to algorithmic discovery, and from broadcast distribution to ecosystem control. Because Zee continued to interpret competition through its historical lens, it optimized for the strengths of the old world while the new world was optimizing for entirely different variables.

The consequence is not collapse but compression. Zee, once a dominant broadcaster, is now one of many contenders in an expanded competitive arena. It simultaneously competes with global streamers for premium attention, domestic platform giants for mass reach, telcos and device ecosystems for interface access, and creators and aggregators for time and engagement. In this many-front competition, its historical advantages remain relevant but are no longer decisive on their own.

For leaders, the deeper insight is clear: when industries shift from product markets to platform ecosystems, the real risk is not being outperformed but being outframed.

The Zee case shows that even high-performing incumbents can lose strategic centrality if they continue to solve yesterday's problems. The organizations that endure are those that recognize when the logic of their industry has changed and reframe their strategy before the market reframes them.

Collapse vs Compression: Two Different Ways Incumbents Lose

Moser Baer and Zee Entertainment illustrate two distinct fault lines of disruption, one violent, one subtle. Moser Baer collapsed because the ground disappeared from beneath it. The physical format died, and with it, the company's entire economic engine died too. No strategic brilliance could have offset the extinction of the medium. Zee, however, was not destroyed; it was displaced. Its domain stayed relevant. Demand for content exploded, and its capabilities remained strong. What changed was the location of power. Platforms seized the interface. Algorithms shaped discovery. Broadcasters lost control of the customer. Zee's decline was a failure of reframing, a slow compression of influence as the ecosystem reorganized around new gatekeepers.

Together, the two cases reveal a crucial truth: disruption is not always about death; sometimes, it is about demotion.

Leaders who understand this distinction can spot the next fault line before it hits.

To conclude, this case is not intended to suggest that content no longer matters or that broadcasters inevitably lose in the platform era. Rather, it highlights how shifts in discovery, interface control, and behavioural data can alter the basis of competition, even when the underlying demand for content remains strong.

9

When a Cultural Gatekeeper Became Unnecessary: The MTV Story

If Zee is an example of displacement—where platforms captured the interface while the incumbent still created value—MTV represents a sharper shift. This is the story of how an iconic cultural curator lost ground, not because its content weakened but because the logic of curation was rewritten. MTV did not face a collapse of demand. Young audiences began consuming more music and video than ever. What changed was who shaped that consumption. Digital platforms dismantled the role MTV had mastered for decades: discovery, taste-making, and influence over youth culture. Where broadcasters once decided what millions watched, platforms empowered millions to decide for themselves.

As we transition from Zee to MTV, it is important to clarify how platform displacement and disintermediation relate to each other because although they often unfold sequentially, they are not the same. Platform displacement occurs when the customer interface quietly shifts from the incumbent to a digital aggregator; the brand still participates in demand but no longer initiates or shapes it. Disintermediation is the next, more surgical step. Platforms not only redirect discovery but progressively remove traditional intermediaries from the value chain itself.

Displacement is about losing the starting point of the

consumer journey; disintermediation is about losing the right to sit in the journey at all. One is a migration of attention, whereas the other is a migration of value capture. In many industries, displacement creates the conditions that make disintermediation possible, but they do not always arrive together, nor do they create the same pressure on incumbents. The Zee story illustrates the former: a powerful incumbent compressed as platforms took over discovery. The MTV story illustrates the latter: how platforms can bypass legacy curators entirely, creating new pathways where the old intermediaries become optional or obsolete.

For nearly two decades, MTV India was the centre of youth culture. VJs set the tone for what was cool. Music videos were curated pathways into global youth identity, and the channel acted as an aspirational mirror for a generation. MTV had distribution power, cultural authority, and the ability to launch artists into mainstream memory. In a world with limited avenues for discovery, MTV was the gateway and gatekeeper.

This dominance was built on the structural assumption that content needed an intermediary. Platforms would challenge that assumption and eventually, erase it.

When MTV Defined Youth Culture

In the pre-platform era, MTV thrived because the youth media ecosystem was defined by scarcity, concentration, and high entry barriers.

Music discovery was tightly controlled. Artists needed labels, producers, and intermediaries. Audiences had only a handful of sources, such as radio, CDs, and music channels. MTV did not merely reflect culture. It curated and constructed it.

MTV's real power came from its position as a tastemaker. VJs had influence. Playlists mattered. The channel's identity shaped aspiration, fashion, slang, and youth behaviour. For millions, MTV was entertainment as well as orientation.

Consumption itself was structured. Content followed schedules. Audiences tuned in at fixed times. Youth culture was shared, collective, and centralized.

In this world, MTV was indispensable precisely because the system required an intermediary.

The first cracks appeared when YouTube surged in the early 2010s. Suddenly, young users experienced an entirely different relationship with content, one with no programming heads, time slots, or curators deciding what qualified as youth culture.

Four forces combined to structurally undermine MTV's model.

YouTube removed the gatekeeper (2010–2014): For the first time, discovery was infinite and demand driven. Anyone could upload; anyone could be discovered, and virality replaced curation. MTV's role as a gatekeeper began to weaken quietly but irreversibly.

Smartphone became the cultural hub (2014–2016): The smartphone moved culture from the living room to the individual. Consumption became personal. What had once been shared experiences fragmented into individual journeys.

Cheap data triggered an attention explosion (2016–2018): With the arrival of low-cost mobile internet, video consumption surged. Jio's entry made it frictionless and ubiquitous. Mobile video skyrocketed. MTV's linear model, which was dependent on scheduled blocks, could not compete with the immediacy and abundance of mobile-first platforms.

The creator economy rewired the value chain (2018–2024): Creators became the new 'MTVs'. Self-contained, high-engagement, and personality-driven micro-brands flourished.

Creators wrote their own scripts, built communities, and monetized directly through platforms and advertisers.

Platforms did not outcompete MTV. Rather, they dissolved the layer MTV operated in.

MTV's Strategic Missteps

MTV did not ignore digital. Its problem was that it responded through the logic of the old world.

Misstep 1: Treating Digital as an Extension of Broadcast

MTV expanded formats, launched digital add-ons, and leaned into youth reality shows. These actions were rooted in the assumption that the channel-first logic still mattered.

Instead of adopting the platform logic of personalization, creator-led content, and algorithmic discovery, MTV doubled down on programming logic.

It digitized television, while platforms re-invented culture.

Misstep 2: Pursuing Aggregation When the World Was Fragmenting

At its peak, MTV had built a unified vision of youth culture—a shared narrative that moved millions together. But platforms fractured that idea.

Youth culture no longer moved as one. It splintered into countless micro-communities, each with its own tastes, language, and identity. What had once been a collective experience became deeply individual.

MTV continued to speak to a mass audience.

But that audience no longer existed in the same way.

Misstep 3: Underestimating the Creator Economy

MTV had once been a launchpad, a place where artists were discovered and amplified. But in the platform era, creators no longer needed a broadcaster to reach an audience. They built their own. Algorithms replaced editors. Engagement replaced programming. Communities replaced channels. The cultural power MTV once held migrated to influencers, vloggers, dancers, gamers, comedians, and niche creators.

Creators were no longer trying to get onto MTV.

In many ways, they had become MTV, each running their own content universe, directly connected to their audience.

Misstep 4: Competing on Content When the Game Was About Infrastructure

While MTV focused on strengthening shows and refreshed formats. Platforms invested in the following:

- Recommendation systems
- Creator tools
- Engagement loops
- Data flywheels
- Monetization pathways

They designed ecosystems that improved with every interaction. MTV competed as a broadcaster. Platforms competed as systems.

It was an asymmetric battle from the start.

When the Fault Line Became Visible

Unlike Zee, which was displaced, MTV experienced something more definitive.

It was disintermediated whereby its entire role was removed from the value chain.

Three structural shifts made MTV's position untenable:

1. Platforms directly connected creators with audiences. The need for a middle layer disappeared.
2. Algorithms replaced human curation. Programming heads lost their influence to recommendation engines.
3. Personalized feeds replaced shared cultural hubs. Mass identity gave way to micro-identities.

MTV did not lose because it made poor decisions. It lost because the system evolved in a way that eliminated its function. Its decline was not a strategic failure. It was an architectural one.

Lessons for Leaders

MTV's fall teaches a deeper lesson than traditional disruption narratives.

1. Intermediaries rarely lose to better competitors. They lose when the system no longer requires them. When value lies in connecting, curating, or controlling access, platforms will eventually reconfigure that flow.
2. In this new world, creators, not channels, are the new brands. The power to aggregate audiences now belongs to individuals, not institutions.
3. Algorithmic discovery beats editorial curation. Taste-making has shifted from human judgement to behavioural signals.
4. Youth culture no longer needs a centre. Identity formation is decentralized, niche-led, and perpetually recombinant.
5. Adaptation is not enough when the underlying logic disappears. MTV adapted formats, shows, and brand

identity. What it could not adapt was its role in the value chain.

MTV is present in India's media landscape, but its strategic role has undergone a fundamental shift. It no longer functions as the cultural centre of gravity for the youth. Instead, it operates as one among several legacy brands navigating an ecosystem dominated by platforms, creators, and algorithmic discovery. Its current trajectory reflects a transition from being a primary gateway for youth culture to serving niche, format-specific audiences across linear and digital touchpoints. This repositioning is not a failure. It is an adaptation to a world where its original function as an intermediary and curator has structurally diminished.

Where MTV goes now depends on how effectively it can re-anchor its relevance, either by building deeper creator partnerships; leveraging its brand equity to operate within platform ecosystems rather than outside them; or reframing itself around experiential, IP-led, or community-driven formats that do not rely on gatekeeping. The diagnostic lesson for leaders is clear: when the architecture of an industry evolves, incumbents must re-express their value in ways that align with the new logic of the system, not the assumptions that built their early success.

A Question for Every Leader

The forces that reshaped India's digital landscape, such as cheap mobile data, ubiquitous smartphones, platform-led discovery, algorithmic curation, and the explosive rise of streaming, were the same across sectors, yet their impact on incumbents was dramatically different because each business occupied a different structural position. For Moser Baer, these megatrends attacked the format itself: once digital access became frictionless, the physical disc had no reason to exist, making collapse inevitable. For Zee, the same forces, instead of destroying the content business, shifted the interface. They turned platforms into the new gateway for discovery and pushed broadcasters downstream, compressing their influence without eliminating demand. For MTV, the identical trends bypassed the intermediary layer entirely. Platforms enabled creators and audiences to connect directly, causing disintermediation rather than displacement or collapse.

The deeper lesson is that megatrends do not hit all incumbents equally. They stress-test the weakest structural layer in the value chain. Yet most organizational planning systems and strategy processes do not labour on these structural analyses. Instead, they focus on budgets, competition, and short-term targets, leaving leaders anchored in incumbency biases and blind to subtle environmental shifts.

This raises the questions every leader must confront:

a) If a megatrend hits your industry tomorrow, which part of your business will break first?
b) Which signals are you currently ignoring because they don't fit your planning dashboards?
c) If platforms rewired your sector's architecture overnight, would you even recognize the shift before your customers did?

10

When Strength Became a Weakness: The HMT Story

HMT represents a very different kind of collapse, one that unfolds slowly, predictably, and almost painfully in plain sight. Unlike the abruptness of a format death or power shift to platforms, the disruption in watches was neither sudden nor ambiguous. The early signals were visible for years. Global markets had already embraced quartz. Consumer preferences were shifting towards design and accuracy. The economics of watchmaking had been structurally rewritten. The technology was proven; the direction of change was unmistakable, and the implications were clear to anyone willing to see them. Yet HMT, the most trusted name in Indian watchmaking, struggled to respond.

This case study is the purest expression of the third fault line: governance gaps, where organizational psychology, cultural attachment, and decision inertia overpower strategic clarity. It is a reminder that incumbents do not always fall because the world violently disrupts them. Sometimes, they fall because they do not act when the evidence is obvious. For leaders, this case is especially instructive. It shows how legacy strengths can become blind spots, planning systems can mute early warnings, and even iconic institutions can drift towards irrelevance when internal beliefs outweigh external reality. As you read this narrative, the intent is not to judge HMT but to help you recognize a pattern that recurs across industries. It is the slow, quiet erosion that happens when leaders underestimate the pace of change and overestimate the durability of the present.

An Era of Industrial Pride

For three decades, HMT was synonymous with watches in India. Through the 1960s, 70s and 80s, it built a category from scratch, becoming associated with reliability, national pride, and industrial craftsmanship. Its mechanical watches were durable, engineering-led, and widely accessible. The company enjoyed the following:

- near-monopoly dominance
- strong manufacturing capability
- trusted distribution
- a powerful public-sector identity

In a protected economy, this dominance felt unshakeable. HMT's leadership internalized this as a permanent truth. The organization's identity, both internally and externally, became intertwined with mechanical watchmaking. Its engineering culture was rooted in precision, process discipline, and craftsmanship.

This identity eventually became its blind spot.

Early Warning Signals

By the late 1970s and early 1980s, the global watch industry was undergoing what would later be called the Quartz Revolution.

This was not a gradual evolution but a structural shift. Japanese manufacturers such as Seiko and Citizen demonstrated that quartz timekeeping could outperform mechanical watches on every parameter that mattered to the modern consumer. Quartz watches were cheaper, more accurate, easier to produce, and far more adaptable to changing consumer tastes.

The shift was global and quantifiable. During the quartz crisis of the 1970s and 1980s, Swiss mechanical watch production and market share collapsed as quartz technology became the industry standard.[15] These signals were also visible in India. By the early 1980s, quartz watches were emerging as a major technological shift globally and beginning to influence Indian consumer preferences. Titan Watches Ltd., established in 1984 as a joint venture between the Tata Group and the Tamil Nadu Industrial Development Corporation Limited (TIDCO), was conceived around this transition and launched India's first large-scale quartz analogue electronic watch manufacturing initiative.

This was not a subtle change. It was clear, loud, global and sustained.

Despite being India's most established watch manufacturer, HMT approached quartz technology cautiously during the 1980s. Company histories indicate that existing facilities were only partially converted to quartz analogue watch production, suggesting an incremental adaptation rather than a full-scale strategic transition away from mechanical watches.[16]

This demonstrates that the leadership did not recognize quartz as the future. It was rather considered a complement to a mechanical core instead of a replacement.

While Titan expanded rapidly around quartz technology and design variety during the late 1980s, HMT remained substantially anchored in mechanical watches. Titan's strategy transformed the Indian watch market by dramatically increasing consumer choice and positioning watches as lifestyle products rather than merely timekeeping devices. HMT, despite having introduced quartz

---

[15]Young, Anthony, 'Markets in Time: The Rise, Fall, and Revival of Swiss Watchmaking', Foundation for Economic Education, 1 January 1999, https://bit.ly/4va6VZw. Accessed on 30 May 2026.

[16]'HMT: About Us', https://bit.ly/4nWIOLr. Accessed on 30 May 2026.

watches earlier, struggled to build comparable market momentum in the segment as consumer preferences increasingly shifted towards quartz-powered designs and fashion-oriented offerings.

This is the telltale sign of governance gaps in action. Early signals were not just missed. They were filtered through old mental models. Leadership interpreted the quartz revolution as a temporary deviation rather than a structural break. Instead of confronting what the data made obvious, decision-makers defaulted to legacy beliefs, emotional attachment, and institutional identity. Governance gaps manifest not as dramatic errors but as repeated misinterpretations of what the market is trying to say.

The Technology Shift

The quartz revolution was not merely a shift in timekeeping mechanics. It was a fundamental redesign of the global watchmaking architecture. Mechanical watches had anchored the industry for nearly a century, but quartz rewrote every layer of how watches were conceived, manufactured, distributed, and consumed. It represented a system change, not a component upgrade. Quartz technology:

- required new manufacturing lines to be built around precision electronics rather than intricate mechanical assemblies.
- demanded a completely redesigned supply chain, moving from machining to modular electronics.
- enabled standardized, modular assembly, dramatically reducing production complexity.
- made rapid design variety economically feasible, allowing brands to respond to fashion cycles rather than engineering constraints.

- democratized watchmaking, lowering entry barriers for new players.
- transformed watches from engineering objects into personal style statements.

Brands that understood this shift reorganized their business models accordingly. Titan—founded in 1984, in the decade the global industry was pivoting—treated quartz not as an incremental innovation but as a philosophy of business design. Its leadership recognized that quartz enabled entirely new consumer propositions like sleeker form factors, fashion-led collections, and high-frequency model refreshes that aligned with the aspirations of a liberalizing India. Quartz empowered Titan to:

- introduce hundreds of models annually, keeping pace with rapidly evolving tastes.
- design slim, modern aesthetics that appealed to the new Indian consumer.
- partner with global design houses and integrate international styling cues.
- build experiential retail environments that were bright, aspirational, and brand-forward.
- scale quickly without the weight of legacy, so there was no retooling drag or cultural resistance.

In contrast, HMT's organizational response remained anchored in the mechanical paradigm. While the world reorganized itself around quartz-driven efficiency, modularity, and design agility, HMT continued optimizing the past by refining mechanical lines, celebrating legacy craftsmanship, and treating quartz as a supplemental category rather than the foundation of the future.

This divergence was architectural. Titan redesigned its system around the logic of quartz. HMT tried to fit quartz into the logic of an old system. The consequences of that mismatch would soon become impossible to ignore.

Governance Gaps That Froze an Entire Organization

When quartz reshaped global watchmaking, HMT's challenge was no longer technological but organizational. The company possessed the talent, manufacturing footprint, and brand credibility to lead India's transition to quartz. What it lacked was the leadership agility to interpret the signals and reorganize around them. The missteps that followed were symptoms of deeper governance gaps that gradually immobilized the institution.

Identity Lock-In

HMT's leadership had been shaped by decades of success in mechanical watchmaking. Over time, engineering craftsmanship became more than a capability—it became part of the organization's identity.

Quartz technology challenged that identity. Competitive advantage was shifting from mechanical complexity to accuracy, electronics, design, and scalability. While HMT remained anchored to the values of traditional watchmaking, consumers were moving towards modernity and convenience.

This created a classic strategic blind spot: the organization confused pride in its legacy with alignment to changing customer preferences.

Structural Rigidity

Structural rigidity refers to an organization's difficulty in reallocating resources, revising assumptions, and changing operating priorities when the environment shifts. HMT's experience suggests that recognizing disruption is not enough.

Although the company entered the quartz segment, it remained anchored to the economics, capabilities, and identity of its traditional business at a time when consumer preferences were changing rapidly.

Misreading Consumer Signals

Post-liberalization India demanded modern design, aspirational branding, and retail experiences. Titan responded with exclusive showrooms, international aesthetics, women-centric sub-brands and youth-oriented labels like Fastrack. HMT, in contrast, relied on dimly lit government showrooms, limited assortments, and minor cosmetic variations of legacy models.

HMT viewed Titan's rise largely as a branding and marketing success rather than recognizing it as a deeper shift in consumer behaviour. The company underestimated how strongly customers were beginning to value design, lifestyle appeal, and modern retail experiences alongside functionality. As a result, HMT continued competing through its traditional strengths even as the basis of competition in the market was changing.

Decisions Rooted in Protection, Not Foresight

HMT's strategic cadence remained trapped in a world of annual reviews, production quotas, and state-run decision processes. Even as quartz technology became the global industry standard and Titan emerged as the dominant force in India's organized watch market, HMT responded with incremental adjustments—cost cuts, inventory clearances, and selective quartz expansion—rather than bold structural transformation.

Governance gaps manifested in three subtle ways:

- Slow decision cycles, with proposals moving through multiple layers of approvals and committees.

- Risk aversion driven by concerns around labour structures and institutional disruption.
- A planning system optimized for operational stability rather than market transformation.

These gaps did not appear in one moment. Rather, they accumulated over a decade. By the time HMT acknowledged the depth of its strategic drift, Titan had built a multi-layered moat across technology, design, retail, and brand storytelling.

Craftsmanship as a Cognitive Trap: A Lesson for the AI Era

HMT's attachment to precision engineering was not a flaw of competence but one of identity. The organization had spent decades mastering the intricate craftsmanship of mechanical watchmaking, and that mastery became the lens through which every new technology was judged. Many successful incumbents fall into this cognitive trap. They believe that excellence in the old paradigm guarantees relevance in the next. However, deep capability often hardens into blind spots. The more pride an organization draws from a legacy skill, the harder it becomes to recognize when that skill has shifted from being a differentiator to a constraint. This pattern is not confined to the watch industry. It is resurfacing today as analogue-era organizations confront the rise of AI and GenAI. Capabilities that once defined competitive advantage, such as manual analysis, procedural optimization, experience-driven decision-making, and even traditional forms of engineering, will increasingly be automated or reimagined by intelligent systems.

Yet many firms remain anchored in past glory, treating emerging AI capabilities as adjacent tools rather than foundational shifts. The risk is not only technological obsolescence but also cognitive obsolescence, the quiet erosion that happens when leaders cling to the skills that built their reputation instead of the ones that will build their future. The lesson is simple: in moments of paradigm change, craftsmanship can be comforting, but it can also be blinding. Recognizing when your proudest strengths have silently become your sharpest risks is the first step towards avoiding the fate of incumbents who saw the future coming but could not bring themselves to act.

Lessons for Leaders

The HMT story offers some of the most important lessons for leaders navigating disruption, not because the technology was complex or the market was unpredictable but precisely because the change was obvious. Quartz was not an ambiguous invention. It was proven globally, scaled rapidly, and embraced by consumers everywhere. Yet HMT's leadership interpreted this shift through the lens of its mechanical legacy, converting what should have been an opportunity into an existential threat. The core insight is simple: incumbents do not fail because they cannot see the future; they fail because they cannot unsee the past.

One of the most powerful lessons is that capability can become the enemy of adaptability. HMT's strength in precision mechanical engineering became its cognitive trap. The organization's identity was so deeply tied to craftsmanship that any technology not rooted in its historical expertise felt peripheral, even inferior. Many leaders face this pattern today as AI and GenAI begin reshaping work, talent and industry structure. When core capabilities harden into belief systems, organizations struggle to invest in new ones, even when the evidence is overwhelming. HMT demonstrates how emotional attachment to legacy skills can quietly overshadow strategic clarity.

Another lesson lies in how early signals are interpreted or misinterpreted within organizations. The quartz revolution was visible for nearly a decade before it became dominant in India. Yet HMT's decision-making systems, review processes, and engineering culture consistently framed quartz as a temporary deviation. This is a characteristic governance gap: when planning systems are built for optimization, not reimagination, they filter disruptive signals through old assumptions. Leaders must therefore ask, 'Is our organization built to amplify early warnings or normalize them?' HMT's experience shows how easily institutions fall into the latter.

Another learning is that disruption does not always strike the product first; it often strikes the mindset. Titan beat HMT in terms of technology as well as its ability to reframe watchmaking as a design-driven, retail-led, lifestyle category. HMT's worldview remained factory-centric even as the industry became consumer-centric. Leaders today face a similar challenge: as AI transforms workflows, customer interactions, and value creation models, the strategic shift required is often more cultural than technological.

Finally, HMT reminds leaders that not acting is also a decision, often the most expensive one. Leadership hesitation, incrementalism, and reliance on legacy mental models turned a manageable transition into structural decline. The company had every advantage to lead the quartz era, yet its inability to confront internal resistance proved more damaging than any external competitor.

These lessons from HMT are a diagnostic framework for leaders navigating the next wave of technological disruption. They reinforce the truth that in moments of paradigm change, organizations don't fall because they lack capability; they fall because they lack the courage to rebuild it.

Thus, HMT's decline underscores how organizations with

a strong heritage, deep capability, and structural advantage can still falter when leadership cannot realign mental models to a shifting technological reality. The collapse was not a failure of engineering or manufacturing but of interpretation, timing, and organizational will. While HMT's story is rooted in watchmaking, its underlying fault line is far from unique. The next case, BSNL, reveals a similar governance pattern playing out on a far larger canvas: a national incumbent with unmatched assets, early-mover advantage and market trust unable to act with the speed, clarity, and decisiveness demanded by technological change. If HMT showed how governance gaps can paralyse a manufacturing giant, BSNL shows how the same gaps can immobilize an entire sector.

11

When Governance Slows a Giant: The BSNL Story

If HMT demonstrated how leadership inertia can weaken a manufacturing incumbent, BSNL shows how governance complexity can immobilize an entire national-scale enterprise.

Unlike HMT, BSNL's challenge was not one of recognition. The signals were visible, the technological trajectory was clear and the strategic imperative was widely understood. The fault line emerged because the tempo of the institution was fundamentally different from the tempo of the market it served.

Unlike digital-first sectors, telecom is among the most unforgiving industries. Technology cycles are short, capital requirements are enormous, and competitive advantage depends not only on scale but on the speed of execution. In such a landscape, BSNL entered with every possible advantage. It had nationwide infrastructure, spectrum access, deep engineering capability, and near-universal brand familiarity. And yet, over two decades, it steadily lost ground, not because the technology was unavailable but because its governance architecture made rapid action nearly impossible.

The World before Disruption

For the first 15 years of India's telecom journey, BSNL was not merely a telecom operator but the country's communications infrastructure itself. Its fixed-line network connected households, offices, and institutions long before mobile telephony became widespread. Its national reach, extensive fibre infrastructure and a level of public trust few organizations could match made it the most trusted provider in a sector still transitioning from analogue switching to early digital telephony.

In the early 2000s, when demand for mobile services began to explode, BSNL was still uniquely positioned. Millions of first-time mobile subscribers entered the telecom ecosystem through its network. Private operators were still learning the economics of mobility; BSNL already understood the economics of connectivity. It enjoyed advantages that competitors could not easily replicate:

- unrivalled nationwide tower and fibre footprint
- legacy-era access to spectrum and rights-of-way
- priority status in national infrastructure projects
- guaranteed customer flow in enterprise, government, and rural markets
- a two-decade head start in brand recall and distribution

However, the very strengths that made BSNL indispensable in the early telecom era became structural constraints when the industry shifted. Telecom was moving from a world defined by physical infrastructure and long planning cycles to one defined by rapid technology refreshes, commercial agility, and capital-intensive innovation. BSNL's governance architecture, which was rooted in state processes, compliance protocols, and cautious risk appetite, was not built for the speed, iteration, and decisiveness that mobile broadband would demand.

In hindsight, BSNL's position at the start of the disruption arc mirrored HMT's world before quartz. It had immense incumbency, enormous assets and deep consumer trust but also a governance model designed for stability, not velocity. As the market accelerated, BSNL's structural design would become its largest disadvantage.

A Fast-Moving Industry Meets a Slow-Moving Institution

Unlike industries where disruption unfolded over several years, telecom cycles shortened dramatically with each generation: Voice gave way to data. Smartphones transformed usage patterns. Broadband became central to everyday life.

- 2G lasted a decade.
- 3G lasted roughly six years, shifting behaviour.
- 4G reshaped the market within four years.
- And before many operators had fully absorbed 4G, within eight years, the industry was already preparing for 5G.

Each transition redefined consumer behaviour, economics, device ecosystems, and competitive power. For an incumbent like BSNL, the signals were loud, industry-wide, globally validated, and heavily documented by TRAI, Department of Telecommunications (DoT), device manufacturers, and international operators.

Some of the most visible early warning signals were as follows.

The Decline of Voice and the Rise of Data (2006–2010)

As smartphone manufacturers like Nokia, Samsung and later Apple reshaped user behaviour, mobile data emerged as the telecom industry's next growth engine.

On 8 December 2010, TRAI issued recommendations on the National Broadband Plan, which explicitly emphasized broadband penetration, wireless internet growth, and national data infrastructure, signalling a structural shift in telecom policy from voice-led expansion towards data-driven connectivity.[17]

The Global Push Towards Broadband Wireless (2008–2013)

As the world transitioned towards Long Term Evolution (LTE), BSNL possessed an early spectrum advantage at a critical transition point in the telecom industry. But while private operators rapidly translated spectrum into commercial LTE networks, BSNL's execution remained constrained by slower procurement cycles, technology indecision, and layered governance processes.

Rapid Consumer Adoption of 3G Smartphones (2009–2012)

Urban data consumption skyrocketed as Android handsets became affordable. Operators who captured the early 3G wave built long-term customer stickiness. BSNL, despite having spectrum, saw rollout permissions, tendering and Board-Ministry approvals stretch across years, allowing competitors to seize the premium early-adopter market.

The 4G Inflection Point (2013–2016)

This was the single most decisive shift in the sector. Global operators were moving to all-IP networks. Device makers were shifting production to 4G-ready models. Spectrum auctions across Europe and Asia were prioritizing LTE.

In India, Jio's 4G-only bet and Airtel's rapid LTE expansion made headlines, analyst reports, and industry forums.[18] The writing on the wall could not have been clearer: 4G was not a feature; it was the new baseline of competitiveness.

---

[17] "TRAI Issues Recommendations on "National Broadband Plan"", TRAI, 8 December 2010, https://bit.ly/4u5cszs. Accessed on 29 May 2026.

[18] Mimnagh, Liam, 'Reliance Jio's Free Trial Strategy: Are "Free" Models the Future?', STL Partners, https://bit.ly/3PLkrDW. Accessed on 30 May 2026.

And yet, BSNL acted on this inflection point only in 2020, six years after private players had already made 4G their core offering. The subsequent cancellation of BSNL's tender reflects how governance obligations repeatedly overrode commercial urgency.[19]

Global Acceleration Towards 5G (2018–2022)

By 2018, international telecom conferences, device makers, and chipset manufacturers were signalling 5G's inevitability.

However, for BSNL, still without a commercial 4G network, 5G was structurally out of reach. It was an entire generation behind the market.

When Governance Became the Constraint

The early warning signals in India's telecom sector did not require extraordinary foresight to interpret. They were visible in global trends, domestic policy consultations, device ecosystems, and consumer behaviour.

Their importance lay in the speed at which they translated into structural shifts. In telecom, unlike many other industries, the lag between a technological inflection point and market realignment is extremely short. A one-year delay in 3G or 4G rollout does not simply mean lost revenue. It means losing an entire cohort of early adopters who typically anchor long-term market share. This is why the early signals mattered: each represented a turning point in the industry's architecture where early movers captured disproportionate advantage.

BSNL's ability to respond to these signals was shaped by its institutional design, not by a lack of insight or intent. As a public-

[19]Abbas, Muntazir, 'Finally, BSNL Scraps 4G Upgradation, Expansion Tender', *The Economic Times*, 2 July 2020, https://bit.ly/3RD3iwL. Accessed on 30 May 2026.

sector enterprise operating within a national mandate, BSNL's decision-making was embedded within a governance system built to ensure transparency, accountability, and procedural fairness. Although essential for public institutions, these principles create inherent friction in sectors that reward speed, experimentation, and rapid capital deployment. Every major decision at BSNL, whether about spectrum monetization, vendor selection, rollout timelines, or tariff decisions, required alignment with the BSNL Board, the DoT, and procurement frameworks like the General Financial Rules (GFR). Each of these safeguards served a legitimate purpose, but together, they produced decision cycles that were structurally slower than those of private operators.

This is not a critique of the governance model; it is a recognition that governance architectures designed for stability and probity can struggle in markets defined by velocity and technological churn. Private telecom operators could pivot quickly, front-load investments, adapt pricing, and modernize networks because their organizational structures were built for commercial responsiveness.

BSNL, by contrast, operated in a dual-control environment where commercial urgency had to coexist with public-sector accountability. The result was not an oversight failure but decision latency, a natural byproduct of system design.

The deeper insight for leaders is that signals matter only if an organization's internal architecture allows it to act on them at the right time. BSNL saw the same data, policy papers, and global transitions as its competitors.

The lesson is not that public-sector governance is inferior to private-sector governance. In sectors such as defence, utilities, and public finance, caution may be entirely appropriate. The challenge arises when governance systems optimized for stewardship encounter industries characterized by short technology cycles and rapid shifts in consumer behaviour. In such contexts, competitiveness increasingly depends on whether institutional tempo can adapt to market tempo.

How Competitors Responded

While BSNL was navigating complex internal decision pathways, private competitors were reshaping the telecom market with remarkable speed and strategic clarity. Operators like Airtel, Vodafone, and later Jio treated each technology generation as an opportunity to redesign their business models around data, customer experience, and capital efficiency.

During the 3G phase, private players built aggressive urban rollouts, secured device partnerships, and locked in high-value data users early, giving them a durable revenue base. In the transition to 4G, they modernized radio networks, invested heavily in fibre backhaul, and pursued large-scale spectrum consolidation, enabling them to offer faster speeds at lower unit costs.

Jio, with its 4G-only strategy, accelerated this transformation by redefining consumer expectations regarding pricing, data consumption and digital services. Each of these moves expanded the performance gap between BSNL and the private sector. Competitors were not only upgrading networks but also redesigning the rules of competition by prioritizing speed, scalability, and bundled digital ecosystems. In such an environment, even a well-intentioned but slower-moving operator would struggle to keep pace. For BSNL, the market was shifting faster than its institutional architecture allowed it to respond, making every delay more costly and every technology wave harder to catch.

Why Structural Design Became the Real Bottleneck

BSNL's experience is not explained by leadership failure or a lack of insight. Rather, it is explained by institutional architecture. The company sat at the intersection of commercial operations and public-sector governance. This duality created natural friction between urgency and accountability.

Dual Control

Every major commercial action required alignment between the BSNL Board and DoT. This structure ensured transparency and sovereign oversight, but it also meant that competitive actions, such as pricing decisions, vendor selections, and rollout sequencing, could not be taken with the speed the market demanded. No private operator faced this dual-control requirement.

Procurement Under GFR

The GFR exists to protect public resources. In telecom, where technology refresh cycles last 12–18 months, the GFR's multi-stage procurement process (technical evaluation, clarifications, financial bids, and committee reviews) significantly lengthened deployment timelines.

The GFR strengthened safeguards around public expenditure, although it also appears to have lengthened deployment timelines in a sector characterized by rapid technology cycles.

Retendering

Any change in procurement conditions, such as the 2020 domestic sourcing directive, required BSNL to cancel and reissue tenders. Each retender effectively restarted a 12–24-month cycle.

Private players upgraded networks continuously during this period, widening the performance and cost gap.

A Cadence Built for Stability, Not Velocity

BSNL's organizational rhythms reflected its origins as a national utility: annual planning cycles, committee-based decisions, and engineering-led cultures.

Telecom, however, had evolved into one of India's fastest-moving industries. The mismatch between sector velocity and institutional tempo created a structural disadvantage that deepened with every technology wave.

Lessons for Leaders

BSNL offers some of the clearest lessons about the relationship between governance and competitiveness, as follows:

1. Speed Must Be a Structural Capability: No amount of leadership alignment can offset a governance model that makes rapid decisions structurally difficult.
2. Compliance and Competitiveness Must Coexist: Public-sector governance protects public interest, but when applied to sectors with short technology cycles, it requires adaptive mechanisms that maintain compliance without sacrificing speed.
3. Awareness Alone Does Not Create Advantage: BSNL saw every major signal, including 3G demand, 4G economics, global LTE trends, and device ecosystem shifts. What it lacked was an institutional pathway to act on these signals in time.
4. Dual Control Creates Decision Diffusion: Shared accountability ensures oversight but also slows action. In fast-moving markets, organizations need to know who decides and who acts.
5. Small Delays Compound into Structural Gaps: Missing

one generation creates a temporary disadvantage. Missing two or more creates a structural gulf that becomes exponentially harder to close.

6. Governance Alignment Is a Strategic Lever: In industries shaped by technology cycles, governance design must evolve alongside market velocity. Without structural reform, even the most capable enterprise can lose ground.

The Five Patterns of Failure

As these stories unfold side by side, a striking pattern begins to emerge. Though the industries differ—media, entertainment, manufacturing, and telecom—the failure signatures look uncannily similar. Each incumbent was disrupted not because it lacked the resources, talent, or history but because it underestimated how platforms quietly transform industries.

What makes these stories powerful is that each case fails at a different structural layer:

- Moser Baer at the format layer,
- Zee at the interface layer,
- MTV at the intermediary layer,
- HMT at the technology adoption layer, and
- BSNL at the governance and execution layer.

Yet the reason they failed can be reduced to just three predictable fault lines: format obsolescence, platform displacement/ disintermediation, and governance gaps.

To make these patterns simple to retain, following is a table that compares all five cases:

Incumbent	What Changed in the Industry	Fault Line (Primary)	Early Signals Missed	Management Missteps	Outcome pattern
Moser Baer	Digital access killed physical formats	Format obsolescence	Devices dropping disc drives, rising broadband and streaming adoption	Doubling down on physical manufacturing and betting on Blu-ray	Collapse: the format itself died
Zee Entertainment	Viewer attention migrated to OTT platforms	Platform displacement	Rise of discovery engines, OS-level aggregation and search-led viewing	Treating OTT as TV-plus	Compression: retained value but lost control of interface
MTV	Creators and algorithms replaced curators	Platform disintermediation	YouTube dominance, creator economy and personalized feeds	Holding onto 'gatekeeper' logic in a world without gates	Irrelevance of the intermediary layer

Incumbent	What Changed in the Industry	Fault Line (Primary)	Early Signals Missed	Management Missteps	Outcome pattern
HMT	Quartz redefined industry architecture	Governance gap: cognitive inertia	Global quartz adoption and Titan's design-led model	Identity lock-in and protecting mechanical craft over market reality	Slow erosion: predictable, prolonged decline
BSNL	Telecom moved from voice to data to 4G/5G	Governance gap: structural inertia	3G/4G upgrades, cheap data and consumer data explosion	Procurement delays, slow rollout and the inability to commercialize spectrum	Strategic paralysis: left generations behind

What makes these cases unsettling is not that they happened but that they happened in plain sight. The signals were visible. The patterns repeated themselves. And the fault lines appeared with such consistency that they begin to resemble something close to a predictive framework.

This leads to a difficult but unavoidable question: if these forces have already reshaped entire industries, where are the next fault lines forming?

Because the fault lines that transformed these companies did not disappear with them. They remain active today, in business models, consumer behaviour, governance systems, and boardroom assumptions. Some industries are already feeling the tremors. Some incumbents are standing directly above the pressure points. Others are experiencing shifts like the first stages of Moser Baer, Zee, MTV, HMT, or BSNL, yet they continue reassuring themselves with the same narratives that earlier incumbents once believed.

Thus, the next part of the book shifts from hindsight to foresight. The question is no longer what happened. It is what happens next.

1. Which industries are becoming structurally vulnerable?
2. Which business models are quietly growing fragile?
3. And which early signals should leaders treat as warning sirens instead of background noise?

Part III explores those questions.

Because in every era of disruption, the most important advantage is not reacting early.

It is seeing the shift before everyone else does.

Part Three

FORESIGHT: WHO'S NEXT AND WHY

12

The Fault Line Fragility Index™

The case studies we examined were not isolated failures. They were manifestations of deeper vulnerabilities. The question now is whether those vulnerabilities can be detected before decline becomes visible.

The first two parts of this book focused on understanding disruption. Part I examined how India's platform economy emerged and reshaped the competitive landscape. Part II explored how seemingly successful organizations such as Moser Baer, Zee, MTV, HMT, and BSNL became vulnerable when fault lines played out. Part III takes the discussion in a different direction. Rather than looking backwards at disruption after it has occurred, we now turn our attention to the future. This chapter is rich with tools and frameworks and, at first glance, it may seem overwhelming, but I attempt to define and codify a process that will help readers institutionalize 'sensing' within their organizations.

The question is no longer why organizations failed, but how leaders can identify vulnerability, detect emerging signals, and anticipate disruption before it becomes visible. The frameworks that follow are intended not as predictive tools but as practical lenses to help leaders navigate uncertainty with greater foresight and preparedness. I hope readers will find them useful.

Measuring Vulnerability before Disruption Becomes Visible

The organizations we examined in Part II appeared very different from one another. Moser Baer operated in manufacturing. Zee was a media company. MTV was a cultural institution. HMT represented classical industrial India. BSNL was a state-owned telecom giant. Their industries differed. Their ownership structures differed. Their histories differed. Yet their trajectories followed a remarkably similar pattern.

Looking back at the stories of Moser Baer, Zee, MTV, HMT, and BSNL, what is striking is not how different they were, but how similar their patterns of decline became.

The warning signs were visible. The disruptive technologies were visible. In some cases, the future winners were visible too. Yet leadership teams continued to find reasons to believe that disruption would arrive later, move slowly, or affect somebody else. By the time these assumptions were proven wrong, the room to manoeuvre had narrowed.

Vulnerability accumulated quietly beneath the surface while performance indicators continued to provide reassurance.

- Market share remained respectable.
- Brands retained recognition.
- Customers continued to engage.

Revenue often appeared stable until very late in the cycle.

The real problem was not the absence of signals. The problem was the accumulation of fragility. By the time that fragility became visible through financial results, strategic options had already narrowed. This observation raises an important leadership question:

If disruption is usually preceded by years of accumulating vulnerability, can that vulnerability be identified before the damage becomes visible?

I have developed the Fault Line Fragility Index™ specifically to answer this question. Its purpose is not to predict the future with certainty; no framework can do that. Its purpose is to help leaders identify where vulnerability may already be accumulating within the organization, even when traditional performance indicators appear healthy. In a world where disruption is increasingly structural rather than cyclical, this distinction becomes critical.

In my experience, organizations rarely fail because they encounter disruption; they fail because their capacity to adapt falls behind the pace of change.

Why Traditional Metrics Are Not Enough

Most organizations manage themselves through performance indicators. The ones that invariably receive management attention are:

- Revenue growth
- Profitability
- Market share
- Customer acquisition
- Productivity
- Operational efficiency

These measures remain important. However, they share a common limitation. They describe what has already happened. They do not necessarily reveal what may happen next.

An organization can report strong financial performance while simultaneously becoming more fragile.

1. A retailer can continue growing revenue while gradually losing customer ownership to a marketplace platform.

2. A bank can maintain profitability while digital-native competitors reshape customer expectations.
3. A manufacturer can generate healthy cash flows while the industry's centre of value shifts towards software, intelligence, or ecosystems.

Performance and preparedness are not always the same thing.

The Fault Line Fragility Index™ therefore focuses on preparedness rather than performance. It seeks to answer a different question:

How well positioned is the organization to respond when a fault line emerges?

The Architecture of Vulnerability

Across the case studies explored in this book, four dimensions repeatedly appeared beneath every major disruption.

These dimensions form the foundation of the Fragility Index.

Governance Capability

Governance capability reflects the organization's ability to identify signals when they are weak, align leadership, and make decisions at the speed required by the environment.

My consulting experience tells me that most organizations do not fail because they lack intelligence. They fail because they cannot convert intelligence into decisive action quickly enough.

Governance capability, therefore, measures organizational responsiveness. The key question is:

Can leadership move at the speed of the market?

I have experienced leadership teams correctly identifying a problem long before they act on it. The bottleneck is rarely awareness; it is alignment. Multiple leaders see the same threat but interpret its urgency differently. By the time consensus emerges, it is often too late.

Digital Core Strength

Digital transformation is often misunderstood as a technology initiative. Digital core strength reflects the quality of the enterprise's data foundations, technology architecture, automation capabilities and decision systems.

Organizations with weak digital cores often struggle to detect emerging patterns, scale new initiatives, or respond effectively to changing customer behaviour. The key question is:

Can the organization sense, decide, and act through digital systems?

Business Model Resilience

Industries evolve structurally, profit pools migrate, demand aggregation patterns shift, customer behaviour evolves, and formats become obsolete. Business model resilience measures the organization's ability to evolve alongside those changes. Some organizations possess excellent operational capabilities but remain locked into business models designed for a previous era. Others continuously reinvent how they create, deliver, and capture value. The key question is:

Can the business evolve before the environment forces it to?

Leadership Foresight

It represents the organization's ability to recognize weak signals before they become obvious. This dimension is often underestimated.

Many organizations possess capable managers and sophisticated planning systems. Yet they struggle to challenge deeply held assumptions.

Foresight is not prediction. It is the disciplined practice of questioning assumptions before circumstances make those assumptions obsolete. The key question is:

Can leadership see change while it is still emerging?

Governance capability and leadership foresight may appear similar, but they operate at different levels. Governance capability is the institutional machinery and includes the speed, alignment and decisional clarity of the board–CEO–leadership system. Leadership foresight, by contrast, is the cognitive machinery—the ability of leaders to sense weak signals, reinterpret trends, and challenge their own assumptions.

In the same way, digital core strength and business model resilience are related but distinct. Digital core strength reflects the enterprise's technical and data foundations. It refers to its ability to sense, scale, and respond through digital systems and decision architecture. Business model resilience reflects the strategic elasticity of the business, including its ability to evolve its revenue models, distribution channels, and consumption pathways as the environment changes.

The Fault Line Fragility Assessment

The following assessment provides a directional view of organizational vulnerability. It is not intended as a scientific instrument. Its value lies in creating leadership conversations that surface hidden risks rather than serving as a predictive tool.

Rate each statement on a scale of 1 to 5.

1 = Strongly disagree
2 = Disagree
3 = Partially true
4 = Mostly true
5 = Strongly agree

Dimension 1: Governance Capability

Assessment Statements	Score
Strategic decisions are made quickly when required.	
Resources can be reallocated rapidly across priorities.	
Leadership teams align around change without prolonged conflict.	
Escalations are resolved quickly and clearly.	
Accountability for transformation initiatives is explicit.	

Dimension 2: Digital Core Strength

Assessment Statements	Score
Data is integrated across business functions.	
Leadership decisions are supported by real-time information.	
Core processes are significantly automated.	
Legacy systems do not constrain innovation.	
The organization is preparing actively for AI adoption.	

Dimension 3: Business Model Resilience

Assessment Statements	Score
Revenue streams are sufficiently diversified.	
Customer channels can evolve rapidly.	
The business can experiment with new models without major disruption.	
Ecosystem partnerships support growth and innovation.	
The organization can respond effectively to format shifts.	

Dimension 4: Leadership Foresight

Assessment Statements	Score
Weak signals are discussed regularly by leadership.	
Scenario planning influences strategic decisions.	
Constructive dissent is encouraged.	
Emerging technologies are actively monitored.	
Leadership regularly challenges industry assumptions.	

Note: The default weighting is equal for simplicity. Organizations may adjust weights based on industry context.

Interpreting the Results

The objective is not precision; it is visibility. Once scores have been calculated, leadership teams should examine both the overall score and the distribution across dimensions.

Organizations rarely fail because every dimension is weak. They fail because one or two vulnerabilities become severe enough to amplify external disruption.

I have created some score ranges as a directional guide, based on my experience. As a word of caution, these are not empirically validated. The objective here is to generate thoughtful discussion leading to decisions that might otherwise have been delayed or, worse, ignored.

Scoring Guide

Range	Zone	Explanation
80–100	Resilient Zone	The organization demonstrates strong adaptive capability and appears well positioned to respond to disruption.

60–79	Watch Zone	Performance may remain healthy, but vulnerabilities are beginning to emerge. Leadership attention is required.
40–59	Fragility Zone	Multiple vulnerabilities are visible. Without intervention, disruption is likely to expose structural weaknesses.
Below 40	Collapse Risk Zone	The organization faces significant vulnerability. Strategic renewal becomes urgent.

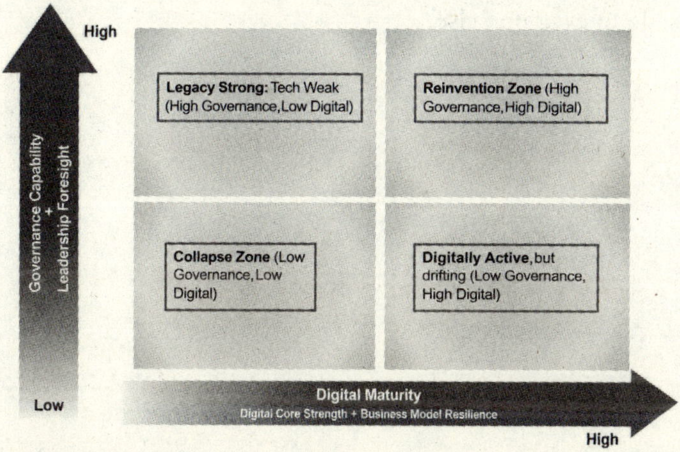

The Fragility Matrix

It might be useful for readers to plot Moser Baer, MTV, HMT, Zee and BSNL within these quadrants as an exercise and see whether they can relate to this representation.

From Fragility to Foresight

The Fragility Index reveals internal preparedness. However, vulnerability only becomes meaningful when external pressures begin to act upon it.

This leads to the next leadership challenge. How can organizations identify those pressures while they are still emerging? How can leaders distinguish between noise and meaningful signals? How can they recognize disruption before competitors do?

To answer those questions, we now move from vulnerability assessment to environmental sensing.

The next chapter introduces the Early Signal Radar™, a practical framework for detecting disruption before it becomes visible to everyone else.

13

The Early Signal Radar™

One of the greatest illusions in business history is that major disruptions look inevitable after they happen. Today, it is obvious that streaming has replaced physical media, just as it is apparent that digital payments have transformed banking. But if you look back at the boardrooms of that period, very few saw those outcomes clearly.

Most disruptive shifts begin quietly. They emerge at the edges of markets rather than at their centre, first appearing in select customer segments rather than in the mainstream.

Because they don't affect the mainstream, they are often dismissed as temporary, irrelevant, or too small to matter. And that is precisely why they become dangerous.

Detecting Disruption before Competitors Do

Another lesson from my experience is that leaders who navigate disruption successfully are not usually the best forecasters. They are the ones who pay attention to the edges earlier. They notice small shifts before they become large and irreversible and treat anomalies as clues rather than exceptions.

It is in this context that I introduce the Early Signal Radar™ to help readers become better equipped to sense the future.

The objective is to provide readers with a practical framework for identifying emerging shifts before they become obvious to competitors, analysts, and shareholders.

Why Organizations Miss Signals

Most organizations are optimized for execution. They are designed to deliver quarterly targets, improve operational efficiency, and maximize performance.

Very few are designed to detect change. This creates an important asymmetry.

The stronger an organization becomes, the more likely it is to focus on existing customers, existing products, and existing competitors—and therein lies its fragility.

Leadership attention narrows. Signals emerging outside the traditional field of view receive less attention and, ironically, disruption rarely originates from known sources.

It often emerges from adjacent industries, new technologies, changing customer behaviour, or evolving public infrastructure.

The greatest threat is therefore not ignorance. It is selective attention.

Organizations become highly skilled at observing what matters today while becoming increasingly blind to what may matter tomorrow.

I have designed the Early Signal Radar™ to counter that tendency.

The Five Domains of Strategic Signals

Across industries, most disruptive shifts emerge through one of five domains. Together, they form the constituents of the Early Signal Radar™.

Domain 1: Customer Drift

Customer behaviour is often the earliest indicator of disruption. Technology may create new possibilities. Regulation may enable new business models. Platforms may reshape economics. But disruption ultimately occurs because customers change their behaviour.

Several years before industries transform, customers start behaving differently in small ways.

- A teenager adopts a new payment behaviour.
- A professional abandons a familiar channel.
- A household begins solving an old problem differently.

Individually, these actions appear insignificant; collectively, they predict industry change.

Before streaming disrupted television, customers were already consuming content on demand. Before digital payments transformed banking, customers were already prioritizing convenience over branch proximity. Before online marketplaces reshaped retail, consumers were already comparing products digitally before entering stores. The leadership question is simple: are customers changing faster than our assumptions?
Leaders should regularly ask:

- Are younger customers behaving differently?
- Are new customer expectations emerging?
- Are customers bypassing traditional channels?
- Are customers creating workarounds that reveal unmet needs?
- Are adjacent categories redefining convenience?

The future often appears first in customer behaviour.

Domain 2: Interface Erosion

In the platform economy, ownership of the customer relationship has become one of the most valuable strategic assets. Organizations often focus on products. Platforms focus on interfaces. This distinction matters.

The company that owns the customer interface eventually aggregates demand and influences discovery, engagement, transactions, and data collection. Many incumbents continue operating while gradually losing visibility of their customers. While revenue remains stable, customer ownership slowly migrates elsewhere. This process can continue unnoticed for years. By the time it becomes visible, reversing it becomes extremely difficult. Leadership teams should proactively ask:

- Who owns customer discovery?
- Who owns customer engagement?
- Who owns transactions?
- Who owns behavioural data?
- Who influences customer choice?

A useful warning sign is when customers remember the platform but not the producer.

When that happens, the platform has commoditized the producer, gradually making it irrelevant, which leads to the next domain: platform encroachment.

Domain 3: Platform Encroachment

Platforms rarely destroy industries directly. Instead, they reorganize value chains. They simplify discovery, aggregate demand, reduce transaction friction, and increasingly position themselves between producers and customers.

The process appears harmless at first. Then dependence

grows. Eventually, bargaining power shifts. The strategic question is not whether platforms exist. The question is whether platforms are becoming indispensable. Leadership teams should examine:

- Dependence on external platforms for growth.
- Demand aggregation patterns.
- Changes in customer acquisition economics.
- Ecosystem power shifts.
- New aggregators entering the category.

One useful exercise is to ask:

If a platform entered our industry tomorrow, which part of our value chain would become commoditized first?

The answer often reveals the organization's most exposed fault line.

Domain 4: Technology Substitution

Leaders often overestimate the importance of technology itself and underestimate the behavioural changes it enables.

Customers rarely adopt technology because it is technically superior. They adopt it because it is easier, cheaper, faster, and more convenient. Artificial intelligence provides a contemporary example. The important question is not whether AI is improving. That is already evident. The more important question is:

Which activities become unnecessary when intelligence becomes abundant?

Leaders should therefore monitor:

- automation thresholds.
- changing unit economics among competitors.
- AI-enabled substitutes.
- new customer expectations.
- emerging operating models.

History suggests that technology adoption is rarely linear. It appears slow for years. Then it accelerates rapidly. The challenge is identifying the curve before the inflection point becomes obvious.

Domain 5: Regulatory and Infrastructure Realignment

Many leaders underestimate the disruptive potential of regulation. This is particularly dangerous in India. Over the last decade, public digital infrastructure has repeatedly transformed industry structures.

- Aadhaar changed identity.
- UPI changed payments.
- India Stack changed trust.
- ONDC is reshaping commerce.

These interventions do more than improve efficiency. They redistribute competitive advantage.

Organizations that benefit from opacity, fragmentation, or information asymmetry often discover that public infrastructure erodes those advantages rapidly. Leadership teams should therefore ask:

- Which new infrastructures are emerging?
- Which barriers to entry may disappear?
- Which moats depend upon information asymmetry?
- How might interoperability reshape competition?

Regulatory shifts often move more slowly than market shifts.

But when they arrive, they frequently affect entire industries simultaneously.

How to Distinguish a Signal from Noise

In a world flooded with information, advantage comes from separating signal from noise. Noise is what grabs attention; signal is what predicts the future. Leaders don't need to react to every headline, opinion, or data point. Their role is to identify the underlying patterns that drive lasting change. The challenge is not accessing more information but developing the judgement to know what truly matters. Recognizing this importance, I use three filters—Velocity, Spread, and Inevitability—to determine a Signal Score (referred to subsequently as the Fault Line Signal Score™). The objective is to help leaders calibrate a timely response.

Filter 1: Velocity

This defines how rapidly the signal is strengthening. A trend growing slowly may deserve observation. A trend accelerating rapidly may require immediate attention. Questions include:

- Is adoption accelerating?
- Is awareness growing?
- Is momentum compounding?

Score your response between 1 and 5, where:

1 = Slow
5 = Rapid

Filter 2: Spread

How widely is the signal propagating? Some trends remain niche. Others spread across demographics, geographies, and industries. Questions include:

- Is the signal moving beyond early adopters?
- Is it crossing segments?
- Is it appearing across multiple markets?

Score:

1 = Localized
5 = Widespread

Filter 3: Inevitability

This filter determines whether the signal is structural and therefore irreversible. Questions include:

- Does it improve convenience?
- Does it lower costs?
- Does it change unit economics ?
- Does it increase access?
- Is it supported by infrastructure or regulation?

Score:

1 = Reversible
5 = Structural

After scoring each filter, consolidate the scores to arrive at the Fault Line Signal Score™.

I have created the following ranges based on my experience. While they are not empirically validated, they provide readers with a useful rule of thumb.

Score	**Interpretation**
3–5	Monitor
6–10	Investigate
11–13	Prepare
14–15	Act immediately

When a signal demonstrates high velocity, broad spread, and

strong inevitability, waiting for certainty becomes dangerous. At that point, action matters more than analysis.

From Signals to Vulnerabilities

Signals alone do not create disruption. Disruption occurs when signals interact with vulnerabilities. This is where the Early Signal Radar™ connects directly to the Fault Line Fragility Index™ introduced in the previous chapter. For every major signal, leadership teams should ask:

Which vulnerability does this signal expose?

Does it challenge:

- Governance Capability?
- Digital Core Strength?
- Business Model Resilience?
- Leadership Foresight?

This simple question transforms environmental scanning into strategic action.

Signals reveal external pressure, and the Fragility Index reveals internal readiness. Together, they provide a complete view of disruption risk.

Institutionalizing Foresight

The next critical question is how to embed foresight within organizations. Most organizations spend an inordinate amount of time reviewing financial results. While this is important, it's rather like driving a car through rocky and treacherous terrain by focusing only on the rear-view mirror. In rapidly changing environments, this needs to change. Foresight must become a leadership discipline.

Over time, I have become a strong advocate of foresight and the need to institutionalize signal detection through a combination of:

- Monthly signal reviews.
- Quarterly disruption discussions.
- Annual scenario-planning exercises.
- Cross-functional sensing teams.
- Executive learning forums.

These are recommendations that readers may wish to consider. I have yet to come across perfect templates that can be readily applied. If the objective is to detect change and act ahead of competitors, the purpose is served.

The Leadership Reflection

Before moving to the next chapter, I would urge readers to pause and consider four questions:

1. Which emerging signal are we currently dismissing because it appears too small?
2. Which platform is quietly increasing its influence over our customers?
3. Which assumption about our industry has remained unchallenged for the last three to five years?
4. If a digital-native competitor built our business from scratch today, what would it do differently?

The answers may reveal more about future disruption than any industry report.

To reiterate, the future rarely arrives unannounced. More

often, it first appears as a weak signal that most organizations choose to ignore. Successful organizations are not necessarily those that predict the future best. They are the ones that learn to notice it first.

14

The Fault Line Disruption Dashboard™

We have now established two important ideas. The first is that disruption rarely arrives without warning. The second is that vulnerability accumulates long before it becomes visible through financial results. To help readers navigate this reality, the previous chapters introduced two tools:

1. The Fault Line Fragility Index™ helps leaders understand where vulnerabilities may already exist inside the organization.
2. The Early Signal Radar™ helps identify emerging shifts in customers, technology, platforms, regulation, and industry structure.

Turning Foresight into Action

Over the years, I have met many leadership teams that accurately diagnosed the threats facing their businesses. The problem was rarely insight; the problem was execution.

They knew what was changing, but they struggled to convert that understanding into coordinated action. The reason is simple. Information does not automatically create action. The challenge lies in converting insight into an institutional response.

This is where the next tool, the Fault Line Disruption Dashboard™, becomes essential. Its purpose is to transform foresight into a repeatable leadership discipline. It provides a structured way to monitor organizational exposure, evaluate emerging risks and trigger intervention before vulnerabilities become irreversible.

Think of it as an early-warning system for strategic fragility. Traditional dashboards monitor performance. The Fault Line Dashboard monitors preparedness. One explains the past. The other helps shape the future.

Before examining the Dashboard in detail, it may be useful to understand how the various frameworks introduced in Part III connect.

How the Dashboard Differs from Earlier Tools

The Fragility Index™ helps leaders understand where vulnerabilities are accumulating inside the organization. It examines structural weaknesses in areas such as governance, digital capability, business-model resilience, talent, and leadership foresight. In simple terms, it answers the question: *Where are we vulnerable?*

The Early Signal Radar™ focuses on the external environment. Its purpose is to identify emerging technologies, changing customer behaviors, competitive shifts, regulatory developments, and other forces that could reshape the future. It answers the question: *What is changing around us?*

The Fault Line Disruption Dashboard™ serves a different purpose. Rather than measuring vulnerabilities or identifying signals, it continuously monitors the degree of pressure those forces are exerting on the organization. It answers the question: *How exposed are we today?*

Together, these tools create a complete leadership system.

Many organizations struggle not because they lack insight but because they lack a structured process for converting insight into action. The Fault Line System™ is designed as a sequential leadership discipline. It begins with the identification of weak signals, translates those signals into organizational exposure, prioritizes vulnerabilities, and ultimately drives strategic action.

The visual below illustrates how the process works in practice and how each framework builds upon the previous one.

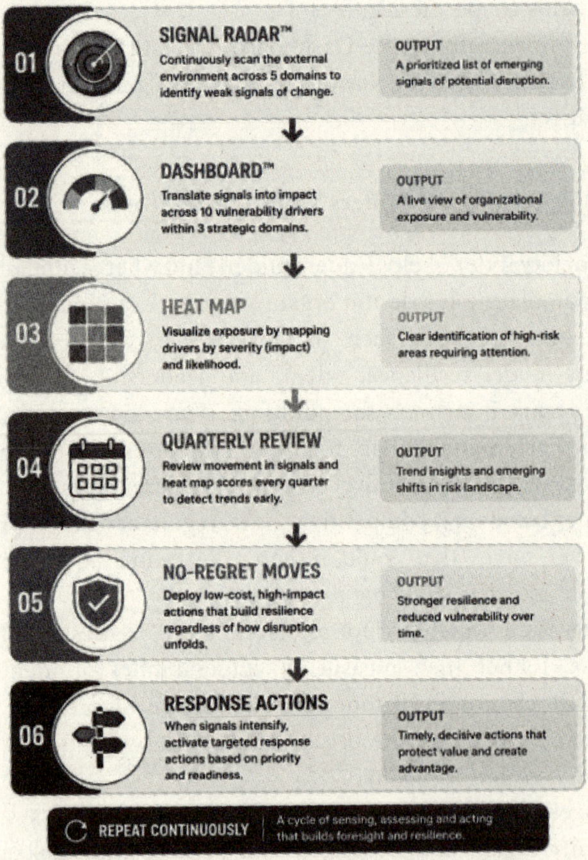

From Signals to Action: A Continuous Disruption Response Flow

Why Most Leadership Dashboards Fail

Every executive team has dashboards.

- Revenue dashboards
- Sales dashboards
- Customer dashboards
- Operational dashboards
- Financial dashboards

While we have discussed this in previous chapters, it bears repeating that these tools are important because they help leaders understand what has happened.

The problem is that disruption is rarely visible through traditional metrics until it is too late. Traditional dashboards focus on outcomes.

Disruption requires leaders to monitor trajectories. The question is no longer:

'How are we performing?'

The more important question becomes:

'How exposed are we becoming?'

The Fault Line Disruption Dashboard™ is designed to answer that question.

The Three Domains of Exposure

The dashboard evaluates ten drivers across three domains. Together, they create a comprehensive view of organizational resilience.

Domain A: Internal Architecture

Domain B: External Exposure

Domain C: Organizational Velocity

Each domain examines a different aspect of preparedness. When viewed together, they provide a directional view of disruption risk.

Consider two organizations operating in the same industry. Both see the same technological shift, and both discuss it in leadership meetings. Yet one responds, while the other continues debating. Three years later, one has reinvented itself, while the other is fighting for relevance. The difference is rarely intelligence; its organizational readiness.

Domain A: Internal Architecture

Driver 1: Governance Agility

Disruption often exposes decision-making weaknesses before operational weaknesses. The question is not whether leadership eventually reaches the correct decision. The question is how quickly.

Assess:

- Decision-making speed
- Resource-allocation flexibility
- Cross-functional alignment
- Escalation effectiveness

Warning signs:

- Excessive approval layers
- Slow transformation decisions
- Leadership misalignment
- Repeated strategic delays

Driver 2: Digital Core Strength

The digital core determines how effectively an organization can sense and respond.

Assess:

- Data integration
- Automation maturity
- Platform readiness
- AI readiness
- Technology scalability

Warning signs:

- Fragmented systems
- Manual processes
- Limited real-time visibility
- High dependence on legacy architecture

Driver 3: Business Model Elasticity

Industries evolve continuously. The question is whether the business model can evolve alongside them.

Assess:

- Revenue flexibility
- Channel adaptability
- Product-evolution capability
- Ecosystem participation

Warning signs:

- Dependence on a single model
- Resistance to experimentation
- Format lock-in
- Weak ecosystem presence

Driver 4: Leadership Foresight

Leadership quality increasingly depends on signal recognition.

Assess:

- Scenario-planning maturity
- Strategic curiosity
- Challenge culture
- Signal awareness

Warning signs:

- Excessive confidence
- Industry complacency
- Dismissal of emerging trends
- Lack of external scanning

Domain B: External Exposure

Driver 5: Platform Threat Exposure

Platforms increasingly influence customer discovery, transactions, and loyalty.

Assess:

- Dependence on third-party platforms
- Interface ownership
- Platform-concentration risk

Warning signs:

- Rising customer-acquisition costs
- Declining direct engagement
- Dependence on external ecosystems

Driver 6: Customer Migration Velocity

Customer behaviour changes before markets change.

Assess:

- Behavioural shifts
- Channel migration
- Generational preference changes
- Digital-adoption patterns

Warning signs:

- Declining engagement
- Emerging substitutes
- Increasing customer churn
- New consumption patterns

Driver 7: Regulatory and Infrastructure Realignment

Public infrastructure increasingly reshapes industries.

Assess:

- Exposure to interoperability requirements
- Dependence on information asymmetry
- Impact of emerging public infrastructure

Warning signs:

- Erosion of historical barriers
- Increased transparency
- New competitive entrants
- Reduced switching costs

Domain C: Organizational Velocity

Driver 8: Technology Modernization Speed

How rapidly can the organization adopt and scale new technologies?

Assess:

- Technology-deployment speed
- Modernization cycle times
- Adoption capability

Warning signs:

- Delayed modernization
- Technical-debt accumulation
- Innovation bottlenecks

Driver 9: Capital Reallocation Agility

One of the clearest indicators of strategic intent is where resources move. Organizations often talk about transformation long before they fund it.

Assess:

- Budget flexibility
- Innovation funding
- Growth-investment agility

Warning signs:

- Locked capital structures
- Slow investment decisions
- Underfunded growth initiatives

Driver 10: Ecosystem Playmaking Capability

Increasingly, competitive advantage flows through ecosystems rather than standalone assets.

Assess:

- Partnership capability
- Ecosystem participation
- Platform-orchestration ability

Warning signs:

- Isolation from broader networks
- Weak partnerships
- Limited ecosystem influence

The Dashboard Scoring Framework™

Each driver should be scored on a five-point scale. Again, this is a matter of judgment; evidence of clear warning signs will depress the scores.

Score	Interpretation
1	Critical vulnerability
2	Weak
3	Stable but exposed
4	Strong
5	Resilient

As always, the objective is not precision but directional clarity.

Leadership teams should focus less on absolute scores and more on trends. Improving organizations become more resilient over time. Declining organizations become more exposed. The trajectory matters more than the snapshot.

The Fault Line Heat Map™

Once scoring is complete, results should be visualized. I have not assigned score ranges to Green, Amber, and Red, leaving this to the judgement of the reader.

Driver	Green	Amber	Red
Governance agility			
Digital core strength			
Business model elasticity			
Leadership foresight			
Platform threat exposure			
Customer migration velocity			
Regulatory and infrastructure realignment			
Technology modernization speed			
Capital reallocation agility			
Ecosystem playmaking capability			

The heat map allows leadership teams to identify concentration risks quickly. A single red zone may not be dangerous. Multiple red zones are. That is how fragility accumulates.

The next step is to establish a disciplined review cadence, starting with the Quarterly Fault Line Review™.

The Quarterly Fault Line Review™

The dashboard becomes powerful only when it becomes a leadership routine. For that reason, organizations should conduct a Quarterly Fault Line Review™. Every quarter, leadership teams should answer eight questions.

Customers: What changed?

Competition: What changed?
Technology: What changed?
AI: What changed?
Regulation: What changed?
Talent: What changed?
Ecosystems: What changed?
Capital Allocation: What changed?

The objective is not reporting. The objective is interpretation.

Identifying No-Regret Moves

At the conclusion of every review, leadership teams should identify three categories of action.

Top Three Vulnerabilities: Where is fragility accumulating?

Top Three Opportunities: Where is value migrating?

Top Three No-Regret Moves: What actions strengthen resilience regardless of how the future unfolds?

Examples include:

- Governance redesign
- Data modernization
- AI capability-building
- Ecosystem partnerships
- Business-model experimentation
- Customer-interface recovery

No-regret moves are particularly important because they create strategic flexibility even when uncertainty remains high.

The Fault Line Response Framework™

Whenever a major signal emerges, leaders should work through five questions.

- What is changing?
- Why does it matter?
- Which vulnerability does it expose?
- What action is required?
- What happens if we do nothing?

This simple discipline prevents organizations from confusing awareness with preparedness.

The Purpose of Foresight

Many leaders assume foresight is about prediction. It is not. Prediction attempts to forecast specific outcomes. Foresight prepares organizations for multiple outcomes. The objective is not to know exactly what will happen. The objective is to ensure the organization remains adaptable regardless of what happens.

This distinction matters because uncertainty is increasing. Technology cycles are accelerating. Platform ecosystems are expanding. Artificial intelligence is reshaping value chains. Public digital infrastructure continues to alter industry structures. In such an environment, resilience becomes a strategic capability.

From Dashboard to Reinvention

The organizations examined in Part II did not collapse because disruption appeared suddenly.

- Most of the signals were visible.
- The technologies were visible.

- The customer shifts were visible.
- The platform dynamics were visible.

What failed was not awareness. What failed was the response. The Fault Line Disruption Dashboard™ exists to prevent that failure.

It converts vulnerability into visibility. Visibility into action. And action into resilience. Because in the fault line economy, enduring organizations are not those that predict the future perfectly. They are those that prepare for it systematically.

The purpose of leadership is not to eliminate disruption. It is to ensure that, when disruption arrives, the organization is ready.

15

The Fault Line Maturity Model™

The Fragility Index™ identifies vulnerabilities. The Early Signal Radar™ identifies emerging disruptions. The Disruption Dashboard™ monitors organizational exposure. Yet leadership teams often ask a more fundamental question:

How prepared are we relative to our peers?

To answer that question, organizations require a maturity model.

The Fault Line Maturity Model™ provides a structured framework for assessing organizational readiness in an increasingly volatile environment. Rather than focusing on performance, the model evaluates adaptive capability. It helps leaders understand where they are today and what capabilities must be strengthened to build resilience tomorrow.

Measuring Organizational Readiness for the Fault Line Economy

Level 1: Reactive Organization

Characteristics

Organizations at this level respond to disruption only after it becomes visible. Leadership attention focuses primarily on operational performance and short-term results. Technology investments are fragmented. Scenario planning is rare. Customer shifts are often recognized late.

Typical Symptoms

- Legacy systems dominate.
- Siloed decision-making.
- Limited strategic foresight.
- Dependence on historical advantages.
- Slow response to market shifts.

Leadership Mindset

'We will respond when the threat becomes real.'

Risk

High disruption vulnerability.

Level 2: Aware Organization

Characteristics

Leadership recognizes that change is occurring but lacks systematic mechanisms for response. Signal detection is informal. Transformation initiatives exist but remain isolated.

Typical Symptoms

- Innovation programmes operating separately from the core business.
- Growing concern about disruption.
- Inconsistent digital investments.
- Limited organizational alignment.

Leadership Mindset

'We know disruption is coming.'

Risk

Moderate-to-high vulnerability.

Level 3: Adaptive Organization

Characteristics

Organizations begin building institutional capabilities to sense and respond. Leadership teams actively monitor strategic signals. Digital transformation moves beyond experimentation.

Typical Symptoms

- Regular scenario planning.
- Emerging ecosystem partnerships.
- Cross-functional governance.
- Improved agility.

Leadership Mindset

'We can adapt when conditions change.'

Risk

Moderate vulnerability.

Level 4: Anticipatory Organization

Characteristics

Organizations increasingly shape their responses before disruption becomes mainstream. Signal detection becomes institutionalized. Resource allocation becomes dynamic. Business-model evolution becomes continuous.

Typical Symptoms

- Quarterly Fault Line Reviews™.
- Active ecosystem participation.
- AI-enabled decision systems.
- Rapid experimentation.

Leadership Mindset

'We prepare before disruption becomes obvious.'

Risk

Low vulnerability.

Level 5: Resilient Organization

Characteristics

Organizations continuously reinvent themselves. Adaptation becomes part of their organizational DNA. Leadership treats uncertainty as a strategic advantage.

Typical Symptoms

- Dynamic operating models.
- Continuous capability renewal.
- Strong digital core.
- Platform and ecosystem influence.
- High strategic agility.

Leadership Mindset

'We thrive because change is constant.'

Risk

Low.

Competitive Position

Fault line leaders

Maturity Assessment Grid

Dimension	L1	L2	L3	L4	L5
Governance	Reactive	Responsive	Agile	Dynamic	Adaptive
Digital Core	Legacy	Emerging	Integrated	Intelligent	Self-optimizing
Business Model	Static	Improving	Flexible	Elastic	Continuously reinventing
Foresight	Absent	Occasional	Structured	Institutionalized	Embedded

Getting started may be a challenge, as the processes I recommend require both cognitive and emotional commitment from the leadership team.

To help initiate the process, I have created a one-day alignment workshop design (Appendix A) that can be run by the CEO or any member of the leadership team. Appendix B provides a worked example.

I hope you will find it useful and succeed in embedding anti-fragility into your organizational systems.

Part Four

INDIA'S RESILIENT REINVENTORS

16

The Reinventors: Companies That Rewrote Their Future

In Part II, we explored how organizations faltered—slowly, predictably, and often painfully—when they misread India's shifting economic architecture. Their collapses were not caused by a single misstep. They were the cumulative effect of format obsolescence, platform displacement, and governance paralysis.

In Part III, we moved from hindsight to foresight—not to predict the future with certainty, but to cultivate a deeper capacity for strategic imagination. Through frameworks such as the Fault Line Fragility Index™, the Early Signal Radar™, the Fault Line Disruption Dashboard™, and the Fault Line Maturity Model™, we explored how leaders can detect weak signals, challenge familiar assumptions, and recognize vulnerabilities that often remain hidden beneath periods of apparent stability. In a world where disruption becomes obvious only in retrospect, the real advantage lies not in forecasting perfectly, but in learning to interpret ambiguity before it hardens into crisis.

Part IV now shifts the lens from vulnerability to resilience. This chapter examines enterprises that confronted the same shifts but responded differently. They sensed change earlier, governed with greater clarity, and reinvented themselves with more conviction. These are not flawless companies, but on the specific dimension of avoiding the fault lines that break incumbents, they offer powerful and relevant lessons.

This chapter does not evaluate the overall quality or ethics of these companies, nor does it present them as universally superior performers. Many have weaknesses, controversies, and unfinished journeys. They appear here for the single reason that each illustrates a behaviour that counteracts a specific fault line explored in earlier chapters.

Nor is this a judgement on companies that do not appear here.

Reinvention is happening in family businesses, public enterprises, digital natives, and large conglomerates across India. This book does not attempt to rank or endorse companies. Instead, it attempts to illuminate patterns.

And finally, this is not a permanent list.

Reinvention is fluid. A company that appears resilient today may face vulnerabilities tomorrow, while organizations absent from this section may emerge as future reinventors.

This chapter is therefore a snapshot, not a verdict. It is a work in progress rather than a final pronouncement.

With that framing in place, we now turn to the first archetype.

Platform Orchestrators

These are companies that escaped platform displacement by orchestrating the platform era rather than being consumed by it.

Reliance Industries: The Company That Refused to Be Displaced

Although Reliance is a household name in India, it is useful to briefly situate it for global readers. Reliance Industries is one of the country's largest conglomerates, spanning energy, retail, and digital services. Its digital arm, Jio, became the primary force behind India's mobile internet revolution, bringing affordable high-speed data to hundreds of millions.

When Reliance entered telecom, most analysts expected

an aggressive price war. Rivals interpreted Jio's arrival as a disruption in tariffs rather than a re-architecting of the industry. They prepared for short-term commercial defence, convinced that the battle would be fought through discounted plans and promotional offers.

Reliance, however, saw a different map.

Jio was not conceived merely as a telecom operator. It was designed as the digital gateway to India's next decade, a platform intended to anchor identity, entertainment, payments, commerce, devices, and cloud services within one interconnected ecosystem. To build that gateway, Reliance executed a series of strategic moves that allowed it to escape the fault line of platform displacement long before competitors fully understood what was happening.

The first was the construction of a 4G-only, all-IP pan-India network. It was a clean-sheet (new) design that bypassed legacy infrastructure and created a network optimized for the future rather than one constrained by the past. Competitors were still burdened by 2G and 3G investments; Jio began where the world was heading.

The second was the adoption of a zero-voice, data-first model. Jio treated voice as a commodity and data as the real currency of the industry. This was years before telecom companies fully accepted that the sector was no longer fundamentally about calls but about interfaces, digital experiences, and ecosystems.

The third move involved collapsing device barriers through the JioPhone which bundled connectivity with affordable hardware. The initiative generated exceptionally large volumes, with over 135 million units sold, and played a significant role in helping millions transition from basic feature phones to 4G-enabled internet access, even though later iterations such as the JioPhone Next received a more mixed response.

The fourth move was deep integration with India's emerging public digital infrastructure. Jio aligned itself early with Aadhaar, UPI, and India Stack, embedding its services into the identity, payment, and authentication rails that would soon underpin India's digital economy.

The fifth move and perhaps the most underestimated was Reliance's construction of what might be called a surround-sound digital ecosystem. Jio was designed not merely as the on-ramp to the internet but as the central intersection through which millions would navigate their digital lives.

Services such as JioCinema, JioSaavn, JioMart, JioCloud, JioPay, JioFiber, and later Jio Financial were deliberately interconnected layers within a large platform architecture designed to keep users inside the Reliance ecosystem for entertainment, music, shopping, payments, broadband, storage, and financial services.

This represented a profound strategic shift.

Most telecom operators focus on selling connectivity while leaving higher-value digital layers to external applications. Reliance inverted that logic. Connectivity became merely the entry point; the real value lay in the services layered above it. Jio became the control point, shaping access, identity, and user experience, and the monetization point, capturing value across multiple categories. Reliance benefited not only when users consumed data but whenever they streamed content, purchased groceries, made payments, synchronized files, or upgraded broadband services.

This multi-layered structure created a self-reinforcing network effect. The more consumers joined the ecosystem, the more attractive it became for merchants, advertisers, creators, and partners, which in turn strengthened engagement, retention, and monetization.

Over time, the breadth of Reliance's digital ecosystem meant that users did not simply use Jio but lived within it. This architecture made Jio extraordinarily difficult to compete against. Challenging a telecom operator is one thing. Challenging a telecom operator with an OTT platform, grocery network, payments layer, fibre infrastructure, cloud ecosystem, and financial-services arm is something entirely different.

In effect, Reliance built an ecosystem in which the customer relationship deepened with every additional service consumed, making the platform more indispensable over time. This is what many competitors failed to recognize. They responded to falling data prices, while Reliance was building a digital economy.

These were not tactical responses but structural bets that revealed an insight that competitors largely missed: the future would not belong to the company with the best tariff plan but to the company controlling the interface through which India accessed its digital life.

Most incumbents saw Jio as a price-war instigator. They cut tariffs, matched discounts, and entered a race to the bottom while fighting the wrong battle. They assumed the disruption was economic, but Reliance understood that it was architectural.

As tariffs declined, competitors weakened their balance sheets while unintentionally accelerating Jio's strategic advantage in terms of more users online, more data consumption, and deeper behavioural dependence.

Airtel proved to be the major exception. It recognized relatively early that the market was shifting from telecom towards digital services. Rather than chasing Jio down the pricing spiral, it focused on financial resilience, network quality, spectrum consolidation, and repositioning itself as a premium, experience-led competitor. Airtel adapted, but many others did not.

Reliance escaped platform displacement because it built the

landscape on which the next decade would unfold. It didn't negotiate for relevance; it engineered it.

Leader Lesson: Platform Power Requires Platform Vision

Leaders must learn to read the architecture beneath an industry, not merely the competition above it. Instead of defending your business against platforms, you must secure your place within the new architecture before others fully recognize that the shift has already begun.

Tata Group (Tata Neu + Tata Digital): The Federation That Learned to Think Like One Brain

Tata is one of India's oldest and most globally recognized business houses. It is a multi-industry institution spanning steel, automobiles, airlines, hotels, IT services, groceries, healthcare, luxury goods, and finance. Tata is a 140-year-old ecosystem woven deeply into India's economic and social fabric.

For decades, Tata's decentralized federation model was one of its defining strengths. Individual companies enjoyed autonomy, developed their own systems and cultures, and built independent customer relationships. As India transitioned into a platform economy, where value increasingly consolidates around interfaces, identity graphs, and unified consumer journeys, that same decentralization risked becoming a structural vulnerability.

Tata Neu was designed to address this fault line.

Why Tata Neu Matters

Tata Neu wasn't just a super-app initiative. It represented an attempt to re-architect a century-old conglomerate for the platform age. Its significance therefore cannot be understood only through app downloads, user metrics, or launch reviews. It must be understood at the architectural level, the level at which industries themselves are reshaped.

The Tata Group faced a growing strategic threat. If discovery, loyalty and customer behaviour increasingly became controlled by external platforms, Tata's businesses, however trusted or iconic, risked being reduced to suppliers operating inside somebody else's ecosystem.

This exact pattern had already reshaped multiple industries:

- retailers lost direct customer access to Amazon and Flipkart,
- media companies lost audience attention to YouTube and OTT platforms, and
- financial institutions ceded interface ownership to UPI, wallets, and fintech applications.

The underlying fault line was clear: once organizations lose the interface, they eventually lose the relationship and often the economics attached to it.

Tata Neu was conceived as a group-wide countermeasure. It was not a loyalty program or a marketing layer.

It was intended to become an interface moat or the missing architectural layer that could prevent the platform economy from marginalizing a federation of otherwise powerful businesses.

Neu aimed to unite Tata's identity, loyalty, payments, discovery, data relationships, and customer journeys into one interconnected ecosystem.

No Indian business house had previously attempted integration at this scale across such a diverse range of sectors.

From Federation to Consumer Graph

Tata Neu attempted something even more ambitious than interface unification. It attempted to build a group-level consumer graph.

In a fragmented platform economy, one of the most

defensible strategic assets is a deep, connected understanding of consumer behaviour across multiple aspects of daily life.

Tata already occupied an unusually broad presence in the Indian consumer landscape:

- where you shop (BigBasket and Croma)
- where you stay and eat (Taj and Qmin)
- how you travel (Air India)
- your health and wellness (1mg)
- your mobility (Tata Motors)
- your digital life (Tata Play)
- your financial journey (Tata Capital)

But these interactions largely existed in silos.

Neu attempted to transform those silos into a real-time consumer operating system, a unified data and identity layer that could:

- personalize experiences,
- cross-sell intelligently,
- integrate loyalty across categories,
- increase customer lifetime value, and
- strengthen long-term affinity with the Tata ecosystem.

This is the same architectural logic that strengthened companies such as Amazon, Alibaba, Reliance, and Grab. The absence of such an architecture made many traditional incumbents vulnerable during the platform transition.

An Imperfect Beginning, but the Right Strategic Bet

Tata Neu's early rollout faced criticism.

There were performance issues, integration challenges, and complexity in unifying diverse businesses under one UX. But these issues do not diminish its strategic significance.

If anything, they highlight the scale and complexity of what Tata attempted:

- integrating over twenty diverse businesses with different systems, cultures, and incentives,
- creating a unified loyalty currency across unrelated categories,
- harmonizing data governance across the group,
- building shared payments and identity layers, and
- orchestrating cross-brand customer journeys at scale.

This was never going to be a short-term transformation. It was a decade-long institutional redesign, not a ten-month app launch.

Despite the inevitable early hurdles, Neu is showing early evidence of the following:

- cross-brand customer migration,
- loyalty adoption across multiple Tata businesses,
- the ability to aggregate offers and customer journeys,
- growing engagement among high-frequency users, and
- perhaps most importantly, a level of shared data infrastructure the group had never possessed before.

These foundations matter far more than early app-store reviews because in the platform era, advantage is ultimately created through architecture, not cosmetics.

Why Tata Neu Belongs in This Book

It belongs here not because it represents perfect execution but because it is one of the most important examples of a legacy institution confronting platform-era disruption directly rather than defensively. This is not a verdict on the success of Neu, but an appreciation of the design and early implementation.

It demonstrates the

- ability of a federation to rewire itself,
- courage to build consumerist own interface rather than outsource customer relationships,
- foresight to recognize platform-era risks early,
- governance shifts required to think as a unified system, and
- discipline required to treat ecosystem-building as a long-term institutional journey.

At its core, Tata Neu is a strategic correction at institutional scale and a bold attempt to remain relevant in an economy increasingly shaped by interfaces, identity systems, and data ecosystems.

Even if the journey is ongoing, the direction is structurally significant and essential for avoiding the same fate as the incumbents in Part II who were displaced by platforms because they failed to build their own.

Lessons for Leaders

A company cannot compete effectively in a platform economy if its internal architecture resembles a collection of disconnected islands.

Tata Neu represents the shift from a federation to an ecosystem and from adjacency to orchestration.

Leaders must learn that strategy without structural alignment eventually becomes theatre. True reinvention demands coherence across governance, identity, data systems, incentives, and customer experience so that the organization operates as one intelligent whole.

While Reliance and Tata responded to the platform era by rethinking ecosystems and customer interfaces, another group of organizations confronted a different challenge altogether: the need to rebuild themselves from the inside out.

Their reinvention did not begin with platforms. It began with internal architecture.

17

Digital-Core Rebuilders

These are organizations that escaped format obsolescence not by defending legacy systems, but by reconstructing the digital foundations beneath them.

They recognized that in the platform economy, resilience no longer depends only on products or distribution. It depends on the quality of the internal engine—the governance systems, data architecture, workflows, and digital cores that determine how quickly an institution can adapt when markets accelerate.

ICICI Bank: Reinvention Under Pressure

ICICI Bank is one of India's leading private-sector banks, famous for its scale, technological sophistication, and influence across retail and corporate banking. With millions of customers and a major presence within India's financial ecosystem, it has long been regarded as a bellwether of innovation in the country's banking sector.

ICICI's reinvention stands apart because it began from a place most organizations fear: a moment of scrutiny and vulnerability. When governance questions surfaced, the bank could easily have retreated into procedural caution, as many incumbents do under pressure. Instead, ICICI treated the moment as a trigger to rebuild itself structurally at the level where meaningful transformation actually occurs: internal architecture.

ICICI's leadership understood something fundamental: in

modern banking, the competitive battlefield is no longer defined primarily by interest rates or branch networks. It is defined by the internal engine that powers decisions, customer journeys, and ecosystems.

And that engine needed rebuilding.

The Governance Reset

ICICI's first major decision was organizational.

The bank repaired and strengthened its governance architecture by clarifying decision rights, sharpening board oversight, tightening risk frameworks, and strengthening leadership accountability. This reset restored institutional clarity. More importantly, it created the conditions necessary for reinvention.

Where many institutions slow down under governance pressure, ICICI used governance reform so it could support, rather than hinder, rapid transformation.

This allowed the bank to move into the second, and far more ambitious, phase of transformation: the reconstruction of its digital core.

Rebuilding the Internal Engine

ICICI did not simply go digital. It rebuilt how the bank functioned from the inside out.

This is where its reinvention becomes particularly instructive.

The bank began constructing what many insiders informally describe as the ICICI Stack, an integrated architecture of decision engines, risk models, customer platforms, and data services that support every part of the institution.

This was not a collection of disconnected projects. It was a strategic philosophy that if the bank intended to compete in a digital economy, every customer journey needed to run on a unified and intelligent core.

This architecture enabled:

- real-time data flows across businesses,
- unified identity, verification, and credit engines,
- straight-through processing for retail and wholesale products,
- consistent customer experiences across channels, and
- rapid deployment of new journeys without rebuilding underlying systems.

In effect, it transformed ICICI into a bank operating at digital velocity rather than branch velocity.

That distinction separated it from incumbents still struggling with fragmented legacy cores.

iMobile and the Everyday Digital Bank

iMobile, later iMobile Pay, became the outward expression of this rebuilt architecture.

Most banking apps originally evolved as transaction layers: digital versions of physical branches. ICICI approached the problem differently.

It treated iMobile as a customer OS designed to allow a user to

- move money,
- borrow,
- invest,
- manage cards,
- track expenses,
- authenticate identity,
- interface with merchants, and
- participate in broader digital ecosystems,

all through a single orchestrated interface.

Because the underlying architecture supported it, iMobile could introduce new journeys quickly and reliably. Many competitors lacked this capability because their systems remained fragmented.

Thus, iMobile became one of India's most widely used and highly rated banking applications. It was built on a core optimized for speed, reliability, and breadth.

Wholesale Banking: The Less Visible Reinvention

While the retail transformation was visible, ICICI's reinvention in wholesale banking was quieter but equally consequential.

The bank built platforms that integrated

- supply chain financing,
- vendor payments,
- treasury functions,
- trade finance,
- corporate onboarding,
- digital documentation, and
- cash management.

Crucially, these capabilities were embedded directly into corporate ERP systems and fintech ecosystems.

This represented a major strategic shift.

Instead of expecting corporates to come to the bank, ICICI embedded banking into the client's workflow, thus delivering financial services where businesses already operated.

Global institutions such as DBS and JPMorgan deployed this strategy, and ICICI was one of the first major Indian banks to operationalize it at scale.

Becoming an Ecosystem Bank

The third major architectural shift was ICICI's decision to participate actively in India's emerging platform economy.

While some incumbents viewed fintechs primarily as

competitive threats, ICICI treated them as extensions of its distribution and intelligence network.

The bank integrated itself deeply with

- UPI,
- API-led lending marketplaces,
- account aggregator rails,
- e-commerce ecosystems,
- ride-hailing networks, and
- digital NBFC partnerships.

This gave ICICI a position at the interface without requiring it to surrender control of the core. It allowed the bank to grow alongside the ecosystem rather than resist it.

This is one of the defining characteristics of institutions that understand platform economics.

You do not defeat ecosystems by standing outside them. You must embed yourself into them.

Why ICICI's Reinvention Matters

ICICI did not simply digitize its services. It rebuilt the organizational structure that powers them.

The bank escaped governance paralysis because it recognized that governance is the architecture that determines speed, alignment, and resilience.

It escaped format obsolescence by rebuilding its internal systems into a modern digital core.

Finally, it escaped platform displacement by embedding itself into India's broader digital economy powering flows rather than resisting them.

In doing so, ICICI created a compelling model of incumbent reinvention:

- governance strong enough to support difficult decisions,
- internal architecture designed for speed,
- integrated platforms unifying customer journeys,
- ecosystem participation rather than ecosystem resistance, and
- a digital core capable of evolving faster than disruption itself.

ICICI didn't run from its fault lines. It confronted them and rebuilt itself around them.

Governance Is Strategic Infrastructure

When markets accelerate, governance must accelerate with them. Leaders who treat governance as a barrier eventually become constrained by it. Leaders who treat governance as enabling infrastructure build organizations that can absorb shocks, win trust, and shape the future.

Infosys: Reinventing the Company Before Its Core Reaches Its Limits

Infosys is one of India's most respected technology-services organizations. It is known for its delivery discipline, engineering talent, and early leadership in global outsourcing. For many years, like most IT-services firms worldwide, a large part of its work took the form of application development and maintenance (ADM). This model aligned well with the enterprise technology architectures of its era.

As technology evolved, however, so did the economics of that model. Cloud infrastructure simplified provisioning. SaaS applications reduced the need for large-scale custom development. Modern engineering practices increased automation. AI and emerging forms of GenAI began influencing how software is written and maintained. These shifts were broad industry trends, affecting service providers worldwide.

Infosys recognized that the technology environments in which its clients operated were transforming and that long-term relevance would depend on expanding capabilities beyond the traditional ADM format.

This chapter does not evaluate the entire breadth of the company's transformation. Instead, it highlights how Infosys began strengthening its digital foundation to participate effectively in newer technology models.

Reinventing the Delivery Engine

Infosys increasingly emphasized automation in its delivery approach. This shift aimed to enhance consistency, reduce turnaround times, and support modern engineering practices. Automation became more integrated into how services were designed and executed.

Automation is now a defining characteristic of modern software development and maintenance. The shift helped Infosys align its delivery model with the direction in which client needs and technology architectures were evolving.

Expanding Beyond the ADM Era

As enterprises accelerated cloud adoption, Infosys strengthened its cloud and platform capabilities. It developed reusable assets, frameworks, and methods to help clients modernize their technology estates more efficiently.

Cloud transformation has become central to enterprise strategy. By building assets and accelerators, Infosys increased its ability to support clients beyond traditional custom development, reflecting a shift towards structured, platform-oriented engagement models.

Continuous Learning as Infrastructure

Infosys has long invested in large-scale learning systems. As clients adopted cloud, data, AI, and automation technologies, the company reskilled its workforce to help them participate in new technology areas.

Talent capability is the backbone of IT services. Continuous learning at an institutional scale helps align workforce skills with emerging technology trends and client expectations.

Stability through Transition

Like many large enterprises, Infosys has experienced leadership changes over the years. Throughout these transitions, the company maintained focus on strengthening its digital capabilities, modernizing its delivery models, and expanding into newer technology areas.

Sustaining long-term transformation during leadership changes reflects organizational stability and governance clarity, qualities that support multi-year reinvention programs.

Why These Pivots Matter

Infosys's actions are significant because they illustrate an organization adapting to shifts that affect the entire industry:

- The classical ADM format remains important but now sits alongside newer delivery models.
- Enterprises increasingly expect cloud-led, automation-enabled, and AI-augmented solutions.
- Engineering talent must evolve continuously as technology cycles shorten.
- Service providers need delivery architectures that support modern, software-driven enterprises.

These pivots reflect Infosys's effort to position itself for this emerging landscape. Again, this is not an evaluation of its overall transformation, performance, or strategies. It simply highlights one element relevant to this book's broader thesis: how incumbent organizations evolve their internal foundations when the underlying assumptions of their industry begin to change.

Lessons for Leaders

Reinvention is often about anticipating shifts before they become visible. Strengthening capabilities early enables the organization to remain aligned with where the industry is heading and not only where it has been.

18

Category and Cultural Rewriters

Some companies escaped format obsolescence by redefining their category's purpose and cultural meaning. They recognized that consumers evolve faster than formats do, and that relevance increasingly depends on aspiration, identity, and cultural resonance rather than functionality alone.

Titan: The Company That Realized It Was in the Business of Identity, Not Instruments

Titan is one of India's most admired lifestyle companies, spanning watches, jewellery, eyewear, and wearables. Titan's rise cannot be understood through products alone. It must be understood through its reinterpretation of what those products meant to Indian consumers.

When Titan entered the watch market in the 1980s, HMT was synonymous with timekeeping in India. HMT watches were reliable, widely trusted, and deeply embedded in the middle-class imagination. They had served a generation well, but the meaning of a watch was beginning to change. Digital timekeeping was becoming ubiquitous on phones, in appliances and across public spaces. The functional core of the watch category was weakening.

At this crossroads, Titan and HMT interpreted the moment very differently.

HMT continued to approach watches primarily as precision

instruments, that is, as tools for telling time, produced with engineering discipline and timeless simplicity. It was a legitimate and honourable approach rooted in the company's ethos and the needs of an earlier era.

Titan, however, sensed that consumer expectations were shifting. It recognized rising aspirations, growing interest in design, and an increasing desire among consumers, especially younger ones, to express their identity through what they wore. Titan understood that people were no longer buying watches merely to know the time. They were buying them to project who they were.

This insight changed everything.

Titan built watches around emotion rather than function. It invested in design studios, aesthetics, branding, and storytelling. It created sub-brands for different personalities, such as bold, minimalistic, sporty, and elegant, transforming the watch from a utilitarian object into a lifestyle accessory. Retail stores were redesigned to feel aspirational and contemporary, offering an experience far removed from the counter-based sales environment of the earlier era.

This difference in interpretation, not capability, set Titan and HMT on sharply divergent trajectories.

Titan was not competing with HMT on engineering.

Titan was competing on meaning.

Once Titan mastered this lens, it extended the same philosophy across categories.

With Tanishq, jewellery became centred on trust, transparency, and modern design. This was a shift from jewellery as stored wealth towards jewellery as self-expression.

Eyewear evolved into an extension of personal style rather than just a medical necessity.

Wearables integrated fashion with functionality, reflecting a world in which data and design intersect.

In every category, Titan asked a question that legacy businesses often overlook: *what does this category mean in people's lives today, and what might it mean tomorrow?*

This ability to interpret cultural signals early, namely, changing aspirations, modern retail expectations, and evolving definitions of value, enabled Titan to avoid format obsolescence long before the format came under pressure. In a conceptual sense, Titan 'left the watch business' long before it diversified physically. It stopped thinking about watches as instruments and started thinking about them as identity markers.

That shift protected the company from the fate that often befalls incumbents: defending a format long after the market has moved on.

Titan's story is not about replacing HMT or outperforming any competitor. It is about interpreting a moment differently and acting on that interpretation with conviction.

Where one company saw a watch, Titan saw a way for consumers to express who they were becoming.

Leader Lesson: Reinvention Begins by Reframing Your Role in Customers' Lives

Products age. Formats evolve. But meaning endures.

The organizations that remain relevant are those that understand why consumers choose a category and not just what they buy. Titan's journey shows that powerful reinvention begins not with technology or diversification but with a shift in perspective and understanding what your offerings represent in the lives of the people you serve.

Marico: The Incumbent That Saw the Future Before the Category Shifted

Marico is one of India's leading consumer goods companies, best known for its presence in personal care, nutrition, and wellness categories. With a portfolio reaching millions of households, it operates in a sector often viewed as stable, yet one increasingly shaped by rapid shifts in consumer behaviour and digital discovery.

For decades, India's FMCG sector appeared reassuringly predictable. Brands were household names. Distribution networks were deep. Customer preferences evolved gradually. However, over the past decade, a different reality has emerged. Categories can shift quickly when discovery moves to digital platforms, cultural trends reshape aspiration, and consumers begin trusting authenticity and community as much as scale.

Marico understood this inflection earlier than many of its peers. What distinguishes its journey is not simply that it modernized, but how early and deliberately it recognized that the FMCG playbook itself was being rewritten.

Rather than responding through isolated initiatives, Marico began paying attention to a series of weak signals that collectively suggested the rules of competition were changing. Each signal revealed a different dimension of the emerging fault line and prompted the company to rethink how it sensed, learned, and adapted.

One of the earliest signals Marico identified was that platforms were becoming the primary gateway for consumer discovery. Search behaviour, influencer communities, and digital reviews were shaping perception long before consumers entered a physical store. This posed a structural risk to incumbents dependent on mass advertising and distribution dominance. If platforms controlled discovery, they could ultimately influence demand itself. Marico responded by integrating deeply with emerging digital platforms—not merely as additional sales channels, but as sources of market intelligence. The company strengthened its presence across e-commerce marketplaces such as Amazon, Flipkart, and Nykaa, collaborated with quick-commerce players, and invested in direct-to-consumer brands and digital communities. Through search trends, consumer reviews, social listening, influencer conversations, and real-time marketplace data, Marico tracked emerging ingredients, wellness claims, beauty rituals, and shifts in consumer preferences long before they became visible through traditional retail research. Digital ecosystems thus evolved into sensing mechanisms that informed innovation, portfolio choices, and go-to-market decisions.

If digital platforms revealed what consumers were discovering and discussing, the rise of D2C brands revealed how quickly those preferences could translate into new products and business models. Together, they signalled that incumbents needed to shorten their learning cycles.

The second signal was the rise of D2C brands. Marico did not view these younger brands as competitors in scale but as competitors in insight. Their ability to quickly test products and packaging, along with their messaging, helped them spot changes in consumer behaviour faster than traditional FMCG processes. Rather than resisting them, Marico learned from them by investing in, partnering with, and acquiring digital-first brands. These moves were designed to create an early-warning system for how categories themselves might evolve.

The earlier signals explained where Marico needed to listen and how quickly it needed to learn. The next signal clarified what consumers themselves were beginning to value differently.

The third signal involved the changing nature of trust.

Consumers, especially younger ones, increasingly valued transparency, authenticity, and specificity, a trend that challenged the broad, mass-market positioning typical of traditional FMCG brands. Marico responded by reshaping its marketing architecture as a more data-informed and consumer-responsive system. Instead of relying solely on national narratives, it began crafting brand stories grounded in micro-segmentation, sentiment analysis, and behavioural patterns visible primarily through digital channels.

The fourth signal concerned retail's shifting geography. The final signal related not to products or messaging, but to the very architecture through which demand was generated and fulfilled. E-commerce and emerging networks like ONDC were not merely new sales channels; they represented entirely new architectures of demand generation. The platforms exposed how consumers compared products, price sensitivity varied across cohorts, and niche preferences scaled over time. Marico used these channels to sell and learn, adjusting assortments, pricing, and formats based on real-time behavioural evidence.

These choices of sensing early, learning early, and responding early enabled Marico to avoid platform displacement. Platforms did not capture the consumer relationship on Marico's behalf because Marico ensured that it remained relevant, adaptive, and present within those ecosystems.

At the same time, the company also avoided format obsolescence: the slow erosion that happens when category meaning changes while incumbents cling to older definitions. Marico recognized that categories such as personal care, nutrition, and wellness were evolving into broader lifestyle spaces shaped by culture, aspiration, and community. It adapted its brands, communication, and innovation systems accordingly before large-scale shifts became obvious.

What makes Marico's journey particularly distinctive is its foresight. The company understood that the apparent stability of FMCG masked underlying volatility. Rather than anchoring itself in historical strengths alone, it anchored itself in consumer behaviour, which was changing more subtly, and far more rapidly, than traditional playbooks assumed. That foresight enabled Marico to evolve before its legacy formats were challenged.

Leader Lesson: Foresight Comes from Studying the Edges, Not the Centre

Markets rarely transform at the core. They transform at the edges, through small but growing behavioural shifts that future consumers may not yet fully articulate. Marico's reinvention shows that avoiding platform displacement and format obsolescence begins with noticing those early signals and having the conviction to act before they become obvious.

Hindustan Unilever: Redefining Categories Before Categories Redefined It

Hindustan Unilever (HUL) is one of India's most important consumer-goods companies, operating across categories that touch everyday life. What makes HUL particularly significant is its scale and ability to sense when consumer expectations are shifting, and reshape categories accordingly.

It belongs within Category Rewriters because its most important reinvention has not been technological or structural but cultural.

Category rewriters are companies that escape format obsolescence by recognizing when the meaning of a category is changing and reshaping that category to stay aligned with what consumers truly value.

HUL exemplifies this.

Its story is not about defending legacy categories. It is about continuously reinterpreting what those categories represent in people's lives.

In a sector where products often appear stable, such as soaps, shampoos, cleaning agents, and foods, the real evolution happens in the changing ways consumers define beauty, hygiene, nutrition, aspiration, convenience, and trust. HUL's lies in sensing these cultural undercurrents early and adapting its categories accordingly.

From Functional Products to Cultural Meaning

Traditional FMCG categories were once anchored in clearly defined functional roles of cleaning, nourishing, hydrating, and disinfecting.

Over time, however, consumer expectations expanded, People increasingly began valuing:

- ingredient transparency,
- environmental responsibility,
- personal expression,
- health and wellness, and
- scientific credibility.

HUL recognized these shifts and gradually reframed its categories to reflect evolving lifestyle preferences and consumer identities.

The meaning of the category moved from 'what the product does' to 'what the product says about the consumer'.

This reframing helped prevent category stagnation, one of the key drivers of format obsolescence.

The shift became particularly visible in beauty and personal care. Consumers increasingly looked for

- broader definitions of beauty,

- ingredient-conscious formulations,
- products aligned with personal values, and
- narratives rooted in confidence rather than conformity.

HUL refreshed its portfolio and communication strategies to align with these changing expectations, helping the category speak a more contemporary cultural language.

In doing so, it helped reposition beauty from aspirational perfection towards self-expression and identity.

A similar transformation occurred in household care. Cleaning products were once viewed largely as functional commodities. But rising awareness around hygiene, safety, scientific efficacy, and well-being began reshaping how consumers perceived these categories.

HUL strengthened its brands around these newer meanings of protection, trust, hygiene, and wellness, elevating household care beyond basic utility.

This reframing strengthened the category's relevance by positioning household care as integral to health, hygiene, and family well-being rather than merely routine cleaning. In doing so, HUL reduced the risk of commoditization, where products are perceived as interchangeable and compete primarily on price, by creating stronger differentiation through trust, efficacy, and emotional relevance.

Reading Cultural Signals Early

One of HUL's enduring strengths has been its ability to detect category shifts before they become obvious offline.

Digital platforms became early indicators of what consumers were starting to value:

- new ingredients,
- wellness-oriented positioning,

- niche product formats,
- premiumization trends,
- and evolving expectations around authenticity and transparency.

HUL used these signals to modernize categories proactively. By understanding cultural direction early, it refreshed category meaning before legacy definitions hardened into obsolescence.

This ability to sense and reinterpret emerging consumer behaviour helped the company remain culturally contemporary even as markets evolved rapidly around it.

How HUL Avoided Format Obsolescence

Format obsolescence occurs when a category's purpose no longer aligns with what consumers expect from it. Categories decline not necessarily because companies stop innovating but because cultural context evolves faster than the category itself.

HUL avoided this trap by

- continuously redefining category meaning instead of defending older interpretations,
- refreshing brand narratives to align with evolving consumer identity and lifestyle signals,
- broadening categories such as beauty into confidence and hygiene into wellness,
- using digital insights to anticipate behavioural shifts early, and
- revisiting ingredients, formats, and claims to reflect changing consumer values.

In other words, HUL stayed relevant by changing its products as well as the cultural lens through which those products were experienced.

This is the hallmark of a true category rewriter. Unlike companies that modernized primarily through technology or distribution, HUL's reinvention occurred at the cultural layer—the level at which consumer beliefs, aspirations, habits, and social meanings are shaped. This is the deepest layer of category relevance because technologies can evolve and distribution advantages can narrow over time, but brands that become embedded in everyday behaviours, emotional trust, and cultural identity create far more enduring consumer relationships. By aligning its brands with changing social values around hygiene, wellness, beauty, and self-expression, HUL strengthened its relevance in ways that competitors found difficult to replicate.

Lessons for Leaders

Formats become obsolete when leaders focus only on products and overlook the cultural context evolving around them.

HUL's journey shows that enduring organizations don't just sell into categories. Rather, they continuously reinterpret those categories so that they remain aligned with the aspirations, values, and identities of the people they serve.

19

Institutional Reinventors

Some organizations avoid collapse not through dramatic disruption, but through steady, long-horizon renewal. Institutional reinventors are systems that escape governance paralysis by modernizing patiently, aligning reform with operational continuity rather than sudden upheaval. Their strength lies not in speed alone but in the ability to sustain coordinated progress across scale, complexity, and changing leadership cycles without losing institutional stability.

Indian Railways: Reinvention at Institutional Scale

Indian Railways is one of the world's largest transport systems. A public institution, it moves millions of passengers a day and carries a substantial part of the country's freight. Its size, legacy systems, and nationwide mandate make change complex by default. Yet over the past two decades, the institution has demonstrated a steady ability to modernize, even within the structured environment of public-sector governance.

Indian Railways illustrates how a large institution can avoid governance paralysis, not by moving rapidly but by moving consistently and methodically.

This ability to maintain progress over a long time is exceptionally rare in systems of comparable scale.

Modernizing Without Disruption

IRCTC's digital evolution is one of the clearest examples of this pattern of modernization without disruption. When online ticketing was introduced, the challenge was not technology alone. It involved redesigning processes that served millions of people daily, ensuring reliability and aligning reforms with governance structures that rightly prioritize stability and public trust.

Instead of attempting sudden, high-risk transformation, IRCTC adopted a phased approach. Online booking, payment integration, and customer-facing digital services were introduced gradually, with each stage tested and scaled in a controlled manner. The result was a digital interface that evolved steadily without destabilizing existing operations.

As India's national digital infrastructure expanded, IRCTC integrated it in a similarly structured way:

- UPI for seamless payments,
- Aadhaar-linked processes for simplified identity handling, and
- DigiLocker for digital documentation support.

These integrations improved passenger convenience while remaining aligned with public-service and regulatory requirements.

IRCTC avoided governance paralysis because it treated governance not as an obstacle to reform but as a framework for disciplined, incremental modernization. Its transformation shows how cumulative, carefully sequenced improvements can modernize citizen-facing systems even at enormous scale.

Indian Railways followed a similar philosophy in freight infrastructure.

The Dedicated Freight Corridors represent one of the most

significant logistics upgrades undertaken in India in recent decades. Beyond their technical importance, however, the corridors reveal something deeper: the institution's ability to sustain a long-duration infrastructure programme across multiple administrative cycles while maintaining strategic continuity.

This continuity, rare in large systems, is a hallmark of institutions that avoid governance paralysis. The project progressed through phased execution, steady investment, and a long-term commitment rather than short-term disruption.

Indian Railways has also integrated digital systems across customer service, operational support, and information management. These initiatives did not require radical restructuring of the railway's core operations, yet they enabled the institution align progressively with India's wider digital ecosystem.

This reflects a broader pattern: adopting proven, widely used digital infrastructure to improve citizen experience while preserving operational continuity.

Such decisions allowed modernization without unnecessary institutional instability.

How Indian Railways Avoided Governance Paralysis

Governance paralysis often occurs when institutions become too large, layered, or complex to adapt coherently. Indian Railways avoided this trap through:

- incremental modernization rather than disruptive overhauls,
- continuity across long-term horizons, even as leadership cycles changed,
- integration with national digital infrastructure rather than isolated technology systems, and

- a sustained emphasis on reliability and public trust, ensuring reforms strengthened operations instead of destabilizing them.

These characteristics enabled Indian Railways to evolve at a pace appropriate to its scale while maintaining institutional stability.

Its journey also offers an important counterpoint to many private-sector narratives around disruption. Not every transformation must be rapid to be effective.

Leader Lesson: Large Institutions Fail Not Because They Cannot Change; But Because They Cannot Sustain Change

Reinvention in complex systems requires patience, continuity, and long-term commitment. Indian Railways shows that even very large institutions can modernize successfully when they build a stable rhythm of improvement, one aligned with governance structures, operational reliability, and public-service outcomes.

What India's Reinventors Teach Us about Endurance in a Discontinuous Economy

Across these stories, one pattern becomes unmistakably clear: reinvention is not a reaction to disruption; it is a posture.

Each of these organizations recognized early signs of change and adapted before external pressure made action unavoidable.

Yet their reinventions did not look the same. They followed different paths:

- platform orchestration,
- digital-core rebuilding,
- category reinterpretation, and
- institutional modernization.

Reliance and Jio showed what it means to avoid platform displacement by building the platform architecture itself. The Tata Group demonstrated how a federation can slowly evolve into a coordinated ecosystem. ICICI Bank illustrated how governance, when modernized, becomes strategic infrastructure rather than administrative process.

Infosys recognized that even successful delivery formats have a lifespan and renewed its operating architecture before the old model reached structural limits. Titan understood that consumers buy identity, not merely instruments. Marico sensed behavioural shifts at the edges before they entered the mainstream. HUL continuously refreshed the cultural meaning of everyday categories, ensuring they remained aligned with evolving notions of beauty, hygiene, nutrition, and trust.

Indian Railways demonstrated that scale does not inevitably produce paralysis, provided modernization remains steady, cumulative, and institutionally aligned.

Together, these organizations reveal enduring truths:

1. Platforms reshape industries, but they also create new architectural opportunities.
2. Formats expire, and organizations that renew themselves early are more likely to endure.
3. Categories evolve alongside culture. Relevance depends on meaning, not merely functionality.
4. Governance is not a constraint on transformation. It determines whether transformation compounds or stalls.
5. Reinvention is not a one-time event. It is a continuous institutional discipline.

Part IV is therefore not a celebration of winners. It is a study of organizational choices.

These institutions did not reinvent themselves because they were already broken.

They reinvented because they understood that enduring in India's rapidly changing economy requires vigilance, adaptability, humility, and the willingness to reinterpret one's role before circumstances force it.

As the book now moves into its final section, the focus shifts from reinvention to anticipation.

The next platform wave is already emerging: powered by AI, digital public infrastructure, identity systems, trusted data flows, and increasingly interconnected ecosystems. These forces will not simply reorganize industries. They will redefine the boundaries among them.

If Parts II–IV explored how organizations responded to earlier waves of disruption, Part V examines the architecture of what comes next—and the strategic questions leaders must confront if they hope to remain ahead of the next fault line.

Part Five

THE FUTURE: AI AND THE NEXT PLATFORM WAVE

20

India's AI-Native Future

Part II was a lab of failure. It showed how Indian incumbents fell apart when formats changed, platforms rewired industries, and governance could not keep pace with technology and capital. The names and industries varied—media, retail, telecom, and manufacturing—but the underlying pattern was the same. Fault lines in the external environment collided with long-standing internal vulnerabilities, leading to often irreparable damage to business models.

Part III transformed hindsight into leadership foresight. Rather than treating the earlier case studies as historical post-mortems, it equipped leaders with practical tools to detect vulnerability before disruption becomes visible. Through frameworks such as the Fault Line Fragility Index™, the Early Signal Radar™, the Fault Line Disruption Dashboard™, and the Fault Line Maturity Model™, leaders were encouraged to interpret weak signals, challenge inherited assumptions, and build disciplined watchlists around the shifts reshaping their industries. The objective was never to predict exactly which company would stumble next. It was to cultivate the capacity to recognize emerging pressures early, understand where fragilities were accumulating, and act before fault lines widened into strategic crises.

Part IV shifted the tone of the book from collapse to reinvention. It examined Indian enterprises that met similar pressures but used them as catalysts for reinventing rather than decline. Reliance treated Jio as a digital gateway, not just a telecom business. Tata began the long, messy process of turning a federation into a digital ecosystem. ICICI Bank used a governance crisis to rebuild its internal architecture. Infosys quietly modernized its delivery engine and talent model. Titan, Marico, and HUL redefined categories before formats went stale. Indian Railways modernized steadily at scale rather than waiting for a transformative event.

Part V now asks a harder question.

If this is what collapse looks like and this is what reinvention is all about, what does the next decade hold for Indian enterprises? Not in abstract clichés but in terms of economic trajectory, digital infrastructure, AI systems, and the new fault lines they may create.

This chapter attempts to map that landscape. It starts by grounding the reader in the economic and technological trends already visible in the data. It then explores a new discontinuity—the move from platforms to intelligence platforms—and introduces three AI-era fault lines that will sit on top of the ones we have already studied. Finally, it examines India's emerging AI infrastructure bets in the form of IndiaAI Mission, Bhashini, MeghRaj, and enterprise AI stacks such as Jio Brain, exploring their promise and the vulnerabilities and risks they may create.

This is not a prophecy. It is a contextual framework for the CXO Manifesto that concludes Part V. If Part III provided leaders with a diagnostic toolkit, and Part IV showed what reinvention looks like in practice, Part V examines the future environment within which those tools and behaviours must now operate: an India that is fast-growing, deeply digital, and increasingly AI-native.

India's Next Decade: Growth with a Digital Tilt

There is no single forecast for India's next decade, but across institutions, datasets, and policy projections, a broad picture is beginning to stabilize.

At the macroeconomic level, India continues to grow faster than most major economies. Official data released by the Ministry of Statistics and Programme Implementation (MoSPI) showed real GDP growth of 8.2 per cent in Q2 FY2025–26, with first-half growth touching approximately 8 per cent, reinforcing India's position among the world's fastest-growing large economies.[20] Forecasts from institutions such as the World Bank, IMF, RBI, and major ratings agencies broadly project India's medium-term annual growth within the 6.5–7.5 per cent range, subject to continued reform momentum and investment expansion.[21]

Official estimates also indicate that India is likely to cross the USD 4 trillion GDP mark by FY26. Looking further ahead, several long-range economic projections suggest that India could approach a USD 7 trillion economy by 2030, potentially becoming the world's third-largest economy after the United States and China.[22]

For this book, however, the more important story is not just the pace of growth but its composition.

India's digital economy—encompassing digital goods and services, digitally enabled activities and platform-based intermediation—has been expanding significantly faster than the broader economy. A report released by the Ministry of

---

[20]'Press Note on Quarterly Estimates of Gross Domestic Product for the Second Quarter (July-September) of 2025-26', Ministry of Statistics & Programme Implementation, Government of India, 28 November 2025, https://bit.ly/49xgOrL. Accessed on 30 May 2026.

[21]'International Monetary Fund (IMF), World Economic Outlook; World Bank, Global Economic Prospects; Reserve Bank of India Monetary Policy Reports; S&P Global and Moody's sovereign outlook reports (2025–26)', International Monetary Fund, October 2025, https://bit.ly/3RHplCo. Accessed on 30 May 2026.

[22]Kumar, Abhijeet, 'Why IMF Says India's $5 Trillion Economy Goal May Take Longer than Expected', *Business Standard*, 27 November 2025, https://bit.ly/3SaOl53. Accessed on 30 May 2026.

Electronics and Information Technology (MeitY) estimated that India's digital economy contributed ₹31.64 lakh crore (approximately USD 402 billion), or 11.74 per cent of GDP, in 2022–23.[23] The report further suggested that the digital economy could contribute nearly one-fifth of national income by 2029–30 if current growth trends continue. Government-backed analyses also project that the digital economy is likely to grow almost twice as fast as the broader economy during this decade, with its contribution to national income potentially rivalling or exceeding that of agriculture and manufacturing over time.

In short, India is a fast-growing economy whose growth engine is increasingly digital. This matters because digital economies behave differently. They are more networked, more platform-driven, and more sensitive to architectural shifts.

A new payments protocol can change market structure. A change in data-sharing norms can redraw competitive boundaries. A new recommendation engine can reallocate attention across an entire industry almost overnight.

The next decade will test whether those instincts were genuinely strategic or merely fashionable. A second wave is arriving on top of this digitalization wave, one that changes not just where value is created but how decisions are made.

From Platforms to Intelligence Platforms

The previous decade was defined by platforms. Marketplaces, super-apps, OTT services, payment interfaces, and public digital rails such as UPI and Aadhaar reshaped how Indians consumed, travelled, paid, communicated, and interacted.

---

[23]"Release of Report "Estimation and Measurement of India's Digital Economy" by Ministry of Electronics & Information Technology', Press Information Bureau, Ministry of Electronics & IT, Government of India, 22 January 2025, https://bit.ly/3PAJCsN. Accessed on 30 May 2026.

Earlier in the book, Reliance and Tata were described as 'platform orchestrators' because they recognized that if they did not anchor the platform layer, someone else would. A grocery or fashion brand that once relied on physical distribution suddenly found that survival depended on whether it appeared prominently within a marketplace's search results. A TV network that once negotiated carriage fees found its audience captured by an OTT app's algorithmic recommendations.

At the time, this represented a profound structural break. But the next break may be even deeper, and far subtler.

The emerging wave is not just 'platforms using AI'. It is about intelligence platforms: architectures in which AI is no longer an additional feature but the principal organizing logic itself.

These platforms will not merely connect sellers and buyers. They will increasingly coordinate agents and engines:

- agents acting on behalf of customers, understanding preferences, managing finances, negotiating services, and making decisions, and
- engines acting on behalf of enterprises, allocating risk, routing inventory, determining pricing, optimizing logistics, and personalizing experiences at scale.

The outlines of this world are already visible.

The IndiaAI Mission, approved by the Union Cabinet in 2024 with an outlay of ₹10,371.92 crore, aims to establish a large-scale AI compute infrastructure through public–private partnerships, initially comprising more than 10,000 GPUs, with subsequent implementation plans expanding capacity beyond 18,000 GPUs.[24]

---

[24]'Cabinet Approves Ambitious IndiaAI Mission to Strengthen the AI Innovation Ecosystem', Press Information Bureau, Cabinet, Government of India, 7 March 2024, https://bit.ly/49tmSS9. Accessed on 30 May 2026.

Alongside this, Bhashini, the National Language Translation Mission, seeks to build a national public digital platform for Indian languages, providing AI-powered translation and speech technologies so that citizens can access digital services effortlessly in their own language.[25]

Meanwhile, the GI Cloud (MeghRaj) initiative is creating a government cloud infrastructure environment that enables central and state departments to accelerate e-governance while optimizing IT spending.[26]

On the corporate side, companies such as Jio Platforms are increasingly embedding AI into connectivity, cloud, and enterprise-service layers. This points towards the emergence of integrated intelligence infrastructures that enterprises can leverage and build upon, reducing the need to develop foundational AI capabilities independently.

When these pieces are assembled, the result is not just more apps or faster platforms. It is a world in which intelligence is a shared infrastructure. Decisions that were once localized and human, such as who receives credit, how inventory moves, what content is shown next, and which claim is investigated, increasingly become the domain of interconnected intelligence engines operating across shared digital rails.

This is the next discontinuity, the shift from platforms that control access to intelligence platforms that shape decisions themselves.

Once that shift becomes visible, a new set of fault lines begins to emerge.

---

[25]'BHASHINI Samudaye: Strengthening India's Language AI Ecosystem', Press Information Bureau, Ministry of Electronics & IT, Government of India, 12 January 2026, https://bit.ly/4vgrXFE. Accessed on 30 May 2026.

[26]'India Building Secure, Scalable and Ai-Ready Cloud Infrastructure to Support Digital Governance', Press Information Bureau, Ministry of Electronics & IT, Government of India, 12 December 2025, https://bit.ly/4uEYDsy. Accessed on 30 May 2026.

21

The Three AI-Era Fault Lines

The earlier sections of this book showed how platforms reorganized access to value. Search displaced shelves. Apps displaced channels. Digital ecosystems displaced traditional intermediaries.

The AI era may represent a deeper discontinuity. It is not merely changing how value is accessed. It is beginning to reshape how decisions themselves are made. The shift is profound:

Products became platforms. Platforms are becoming intelligence systems.

In an AI-native India, the earlier fault lines will not disappear. They will evolve into new forms of vulnerability.

The First AI-Era Fault Line: Agentic Disintermediation

During the platform decade, competition revolved around app icons, search rankings, and home-screen placement. In the intelligence decade, however, the primary interface may belong to an autonomous agent acting on behalf of the customer.

Imagine a near-future customer in urban India or, increasingly, in a smaller town using a smartphone and voice interface who no longer begins with Open Amazon or Open XYZ Bank. Instead, they simply say, 'Find me a 350-litre fridge under ₹40,000 that uses the least electricity and can be delivered by Sunday.' 'Rebalance my investments if interest rates are expected to rise next quarter.' 'Translate this medical report and tell me what questions I should ask my doctor.'

The agent interprets the intent and interacts across multiple platforms. It understands the customer's preferences, history, language, and risk profile. It negotiates across retailers, banks, media providers, insurers, and even government services. In such a world, loyalty may increasingly belong to the agent than to any individual platform.

For retailers that already ceded discovery to marketplaces, this creates a second layer of distance. The agent may treat brands as interchangeable suppliers that simply need to meet a set of constraints.

For banks that already lost payments visibility to UPI apps, the shift becomes even more significant. The agent may optimize continuously across institutions for rates, convenience, safety, and service quality, reducing banks to invisible infrastructure layers. For media companies that already lost scheduled prime-time attention to OTT ecosystems, the agent may select individual pieces of content across services, further eroding the very notion of a 'channel'.

This changes the economics of competition. During the platform era, brands fought to be discovered. During the intelligence era, they may fight to be selected by agents acting on behalf of customers.

The question shifts from:

Can customers find us?

to

Will the agent choose us?

In retrospect, many of the reinventors discussed in Part IV were already rehearsing for this world, even if they did not describe it in those terms. Reliance's insistence on positioning Jio as a gateway into digital life, Tata's effort to create Neu as a group-level interface, and Titan's emphasis on identity and emotional meaning rather than product specifications all reflected a similar instinct, 'We must remain relevant before the algorithm makes its decision, not only afterwards.'

Leaders should therefore ask:

If intelligent agents become the customer's primary interface, what remains uniquely ours?

Brand? Trust? Ecosystem reach? Proprietary capabilities? Or are we becoming invisible infrastructure?

The Second AI-Era Fault Line: Intelligence Readiness

AI is not magic; it is fundamentally dependent on patterns extracted from data. The more timely, granular, and well-governed an organization's data systems are, the more effectively its intelligence engines can function. Conversely, fragmented, low-quality, or poorly governed data environments cause AI systems either to underperform or behave unpredictably.

Many of the collapses explored in Part II were already, quietly, data stories. Companies that appeared powerful on the outside turned out to have very little digital visibility on the inside.

In the AI era, intelligence itself may become increasingly accessible through public infrastructure and commercial ecosystems. The differentiator will not necessarily be access to models. It will be organizational readiness: data quality, governance discipline, process integration, and institutional trust.

When intelligence becomes abundant, preparedness becomes scarce.

By contrast, several of the reinventors in Part IV had spent years integrating and modernizing their data foundations. ICICI Bank's integrated stack enabled a more holistic understanding of customers and risk. Infosys created systems capable of connecting skills, delivery, workflows, and automation at scale. Indian Railways modernized progressively, creating common digital platforms across bookings, freight, and payments without destabilizing operations.

The arrival of IndiaAI, Bhashini, and MeghRaj heightens this fault line. When compute infrastructure, foundational models, and language systems are available 'as a service', the question is no longer, 'Do you have access to AI?' It is, 'Is your governance and data architecture mature enough to leverage AI meaningfully, responsibly, and safely?'

A bank that cannot reconcile basic customer data across its systems will not suddenly become intelligent because national AI infrastructure exists. A hospital network with weak consent mechanisms and poor-quality records will not be redeemed by diagnostic AI.

The Third AI-Era Fault Line: Engine Dependence

The third fault line concerns engines. In the intelligence-platform era, the core unit of power is no longer the standalone product or app. It is the engine: the pricing engine, recommendation engine, logistics engine, underwriting engine, fraud-detection engine, and triage engine. These systems increasingly determine what is shown, what is prioritized, who receives access, how risk is allocated, and at what price decisions are made.

The defining feature of engines is scale. A mis-designed pricing engine does not make a mistake once; it makes the same mistake across millions of transactions. A well-designed logistics engine does not merely reduce costs marginally; it fundamentally reshapes reliability, speed, and network efficiency.

The early forms of this logic were already visible in Part IV. ICICI Bank's integrated stack automated certain kinds of decisions. Infosys moved from human-only project planning to a more systematic, data-driven approach to work. Marico and HUL built continuous learning loops around digital behavioural signals rather than treating them merely as campaign outputs. None of these systems were explicitly labelled AI engines, but the mindset was similar: build reusable systems that improve continuously beneath visible products and interfaces.

What is new now is that these engines can increasingly be rented as services. IndiaAI's compute infrastructure, Bhashini's language APIs, MeghRaj's cloud environment and private MLaaS ecosystems such as Jio Brain create a landscape in which even mid-sized firms can deploy sophisticated intelligence capabilities without owning the full stack. Although this is liberating, it raises a strategic question: whose engines are you operating on, and what does that do to your independence?

Put differently, the AI-era risk is not only that customers may be intermediated by platforms or agents. It is that your own decisions may be intermediated by external engines whose incentives, priorities, and optimization logic you do not fully control.

From Platform Era to Intelligence Era

Platform Era	**Intelligence Era**
Discovery	Delegation
Apps	Agents
Search rankings	Agent selection
User interfaces	Conversational interfaces
Data accumulation	Intelligence readiness
Product ownership	Engine orchestration
Human decisions	Engine-assisted decisions
Platform dependence	Engine dependence

The strategic challenge for leaders is therefore not merely adopting AI. It is redesigning their organizations for a world in which intelligence itself becomes infrastructural.

These fault lines, however, will not unfold in a vacuum. They will emerge within the institutional architecture that India is actively constructing for the AI era. The country's choices about compute, language systems, cloud infrastructure, and public digital goods will shape who gains access to intelligence, who captures value, and where accountability ultimately resides. To understand the future of these fault lines, we must therefore understand the infrastructure beneath them.

India's AI Infrastructure: The New Arena of Competition

Seen through this lens, India's AI initiatives are not only technology projects but also governance choices that will shape where power resides in the coming decade.

The IndiaAI Mission aims to position AI infrastructure as a public good. According to the mission's stated objectives, it seeks to 'catalyse India's AI ecosystem' by democratizing access to computing infrastructure and enabling broader participation in AI innovation beyond a small group of well-capitalized firms.[27]

If it works as designed, IndiaAI could play the same role for AI that UPI played for payments: lowering barriers to entry, reducing dependence on expensive proprietary infrastructure, and enabling broader experimentation and competition. But the risks are equally significant. Public AI infrastructure may remain underutilized if access frameworks are rigid or poorly designed. It may also become concentrated if a small set of powerful players dominate compute access and corner most of

[27]'IndiaAI Mission', India AI, https://bit.ly/4fhdHrD. Accessed on 30 May 2026.

the capacity. If foundational models trained on national datasets embed systematic biases, those biases could propagate across multiple industries simultaneously. And if governance evolves too slowly, infrastructure that was meant to accelerate innovation may itself become a bottleneck.

Bhashini, meanwhile, tries to solve a distinctly Indian challenge: language fragmentation. It seeks to build a national public digital platform for languages, providing translation, speech-recognition, and speech-synthesis models accessible via APIs so that public and private services can reach citizens in their own language and dialects. In principle, this can be transformative. A small farmer, a first-time internet user in a tier-3 city or a senior citizen speaking only a regional language could theoretically interact with digital services and AI systems without being forced into English or Hindi.

If successful, Bhashini could make language access a shared utility rather than a competitive moat. However, it also opens a new attack surface: deepfake audio, AI-enabled fraud, persuasive scams, and misinformation campaigns in multiple Indian languages. It also exposes internal fragilities: a bank or insurer that once claimed vernacular outreach as a differentiator will find that others can match that quickly. The real differentiation will move to behavioural understanding, trust, and decision quality in addition to the language layer, areas where many incumbents remain underprepared.

The GI Cloud (MeghRaj) initiative is more understated but equally important. By creating a national cloud environment for government departments and by empanelling multiple cloud service providers under common standards, it aims to accelerate e-governance, digital payments, identity verification, and consent-based data sharing while optimizing IT spend. Over time, such environments may become natural homes for machine-learning workloads involving fraud detection, citizen-service triage, document intelligence, and large-scale public-data analysis.

For PSU-heavy sectors and state-linked enterprises, this is an opportunity to leapfrog without building everything themselves. For private incumbents who assumed that public institutions would always be technologically weak, it is a warning that the state can become a digitally competent competitor or orchestrator, not just a regulator.

On the corporate side, platforms such as Jio Brain illustrate how private players will build their own intelligence platforms. They promise to help enterprises embed AI into operations, from customer engagement to document processing, without massive upfront investment. That can be powerful for a mid-sized company that wants to modernize quickly. But it also raises questions about dependence. If your core intelligence engines run on someone else's platform, what happens when their priorities, pricing, policies, or incentives change?

Together, IndiaAI, Bhashini, MeghRaj, and private MLaaS ecosystems suggest that India is not leaving AI adoption entirely to market forces. It is building AI as infrastructure. That could make the next wave of disruption more inclusive. It could also concentrate a great deal of influence within the institutions that design, govern, and own these infrastructures.

For leaders reading this book, the strategic implication is that you will not be competing in a neutral, technology-agnostic field. You will be competing inside an India shaped by deliberate AI infrastructure choices.

Why This Matters for Leaders

At this point, it is reasonable for the reader to ask why spend so much time discussing macroeconomic trends, public AI missions, and hypothetical agents? How does any of this help a CXO dealing with quarterly pressures in BFSI, retail, manufacturing, healthcare, or public services?

The answer lies in the structure of the book.

Part II showed that incumbents rarely collapse because of a single mistake. They fail when external fault lines collide with vulnerabilities that have accumulated internally for years. Part III gave leaders a method to uncover those vulnerabilities before it is too late. Part IV demonstrated that it is possible even in India and in complex sectors to respond differently, by reading structural shifts early, investing in governance and data foundations, and redefining categories before they lose relevance.

The first segment of Part V is about the environment within which leaders will operate over the next decade. It explains:

1) how India's economy and digital infrastructure are evolving,
2) how platforms are becoming intelligence platforms,
3) how new AI-era fault lines will layer themselves on top of earlier ones, and
4) how India's AI infrastructure bets may reshape the competitive landscape—including the risks embedded within them.

The next chapter turns these ideas into a practical leadership framework: the CXO Manifesto.

It distils everything explored in this book, from institutional collapse to reinvention, from fragility diagnostics to AI-era fault lines, into a set of organizational disciplines. These are not abstract leadership virtues. They are design choices that, if taken seriously, determine whether organizations drift towards fragility or build the capacity for endurance and reinvention.

22

The CXO Manifesto

The idea of a manifesto may sound dramatic, but this book shows that the difference between collapse and reinvention is often not a single brilliant strategy but a set of stubborn behaviours.

Endurance, in this context, does not mean permanence or resistance to change. It means preserving relevance through repeated reinvention. Organizations endure not because they remain unchanged but because they continuously adapt before their vulnerabilities harden into crises.

These behaviours can be described as disciplines or practices that leaders choose to repeat until they become part of the organization's reflexes. In this section, we describe five such disciplines that matter for creating enduring enterprises, especially in an AI-native India.

They are the disciplines of

- owning the interface,
- building an identity graph rather than a points-based loyalty program,
- governing at market speed,
- shifting from ownership to orchestration, and
- building engines, not just experiments.

Each one is grounded in the stories you have already encountered in Parts II, III, and IV. Each one is sharpened by the future we have just explored.

Owning the Interface

Every major collapse in this book has some version of interface loss at its core. The retailer that once owned the high street found itself reduced to a tile inside a marketplace grid. The TV network that once owned the evening slot saw its viewers pulled away by an OTT app. The bank that once owned the customer's pay slip and savings book watched as payment apps stepped between it and its customers' daily financial lives.

Conversely, the most successful reinventors deliberately tried to claw back interface power. Jio offered cheap data and complemented it with apps, content, devices, payments, and cloud services so that citizens and enterprises encountered Jio at multiple touchpoints. The intention of Tata Neu is clear: a Tata customer should not have to start with an external super-app to access Tata's services.

In the AI decade, the interface is becoming even more elusive. The primary interface may increasingly be an agent, a system that understands the user, formulates requests, and interacts with multiple services on their behalf.

For a CXO, the question is no longer, 'How many monthly active users does our app have?' It is, 'In a world where agents mediate attention and choice, in what moments and in what ways do we still matter?'

Owning the interface does not necessarily mean owning the app. It could mean ensuring that your brand is the default recommendation an agent prefers in certain contexts because it has learned that you are the safest or most reliable choice. It could mean building your own specialized agent for a specific domain, such as a health advisory agent that patients trust or a small business finance agent that entrepreneurs rely upon. It could also mean creating an offline–online service journey in which human touch and digital convenience reinforce each other rather than compete.

Discipline means treating the interface as a strategic asset, not as a side effect of marketing. It means being explicit in leadership conversations about where and how the organization intends to engage customers in a world where AI systems will increasingly influence what gets surfaced and what remains hidden.

Building an Identity Graph

It is tempting to respond to platform- and agent-mediated worlds with familiar tools like loyalty programs, cashbacks, and points. For a while, these tactics can create stickiness, but they are not the same as understanding the customer.

An identity graph is a different kind of asset. It is a continually updated picture of how a person or entity behaves across your ecosystem: what they buy, in what sequence, through which channels, with what outcomes, and at what moments in life. It links identifiers across products and services and learns from events rather than quarterly aggregates.

In the reinvention stories, you saw fragments of this approach. Tata's ambition with Neu was not just to cross-sell but to understand a Tata customer across groceries, travel, fashion, financial services, and healthcare. ICICI Bank's rebuilt stack made it possible to see a customer's relationships holistically rather than as unrelated accounts. Consumer companies like Marico and HUL used digital data as a lens to see emerging behaviours and meanings.

In an AI-native environment, an identity graph is the substrate on which pricing engines, risk engines, and recommendation engines operate. Without it, those engines will either generalize too crudely or overfit small pockets of data. With it, they can learn and adapt.

For leadership, the discipline is twofold. First is to treat identity and data architecture as board-level concerns rather than technical details. Someone senior must take responsibility for the coherence and quality of the organization's identity graph. Second is to invest steadily in cleaning, linking, and enriching data even when there is no immediate 'AI use case' that justifies the cost. As the reinventors show, those who invested early in data foundations were able to move fast when new technologies became available.

Governing at Market Speed

Governance featured heavily in the earlier parts of this book and for good reason. We repeatedly saw that the outward signs of trouble, such as missed quarters, market-share loss, and public disputes, arrived long after internal warning lights had begun flashing.

ICICI Bank's story, for instance, begins with a governance challenge. The bank's leaders responded with crisis communication as well as a deep re-examination of how decisions were made, risks were surfaced, and the internal engine was structured. Infosys, through multiple leadership transitions, maintained a commitment to improving its delivery model and talent systems rather than freezing in uncertainty. Indian Railways, despite being a vast public institution, found ways to move in steady, incremental steps on safety, capacity, and digitalization.

In an AI era, governance becomes more complex. Decisions can now be delegated to models that are opaque even to their creators. Mistakes can scale rapidly. Biases can enter quietly via data and propagate across systems. Regulatory expectations are still evolving.

To govern at market speed does not mean rushing or bypassing safeguards. It means ensuring that the feedback loop encompassing external signals, internal insights, and formal decision-making is short enough to matter. It means using tools like the Fragility Matrix as standing inputs into board and executive discussions. It means being explicit about which AI systems are allowed to act autonomously, under what constraints, with what monitoring and with what human override mechanisms.

Most importantly, it means accepting that governance itself is a capability that must be modernized. Committees, policies, and reporting structures designed for a slower, analogue world will not magically adapt to supervising AI engines. They must be redesigned carefully but decisively to handle a new volume and velocity of decisions.

Orchestrating Ecosystems

One of the undercurrents in Part IV was a shift in how reinventors thought about control. Reliance did not try to own every supplier, creator, or seller on its platforms. Rather, it tried to shape the environment in which they operated. Tata, with Neu, was experimenting with how to align many independently governed businesses under a loose digital umbrella. Even Indian Railways, with its mix of public and private partnerships in freight and services, was learning to be an orchestrator as much as an operator.

The AI-native India described before pushes this logic further. Intelligence platforms, agents, and open networks naturally favour modular ecosystems over closed monoliths. Engines can coordinate many small providers. Public digital infrastructure makes interoperability easier. Customers are becoming less patient with institutions that try to lock them into single-vendor worlds.

For leaders, this implies a shift from asking, 'What do we own?' to asking, 'What do we orchestrate?

Orchestration can take many forms. It can mean designing standards and APIs that make it easy for partners to plug into your systems while ensuring that data flows and economics remain fair. It can mean using your identity graph to create value for partners as well as yourself. It can mean accepting that some value will be created at the edges of your ecosystem, beyond your direct control, and focusing instead on the health of the network.

This does not mean that large enterprises should weaken themselves. Rather, in a world driven by intelligence platforms, the strongest organizations are often those that shape ecosystems and interactions instead of owning every asset themselves. Success increasingly depends on building models and governance systems that reward collaboration, network strength, resilience, and fair value creation, not just asset ownership or utilization.

Building Engines

The final discipline brings us back to the engines. For many organizations today, AI sits in a corner labelled innovation with proofs-of-concept, pilots, and small projects. That is understandable because experimentation is how learning begins. However, if AI remains trapped in that corner, it will never reshape the enterprise's economics or resilience.

The reinventors in Part IV did not talk about AI use cases in the language of hype cycles. They made quiet, structural moves. ICICI Bank invested in a unified decision and journey platform. Infosys re-engineered how work flowed and how skills were developed. Consumer companies leveraged digital channels as sensing mechanisms for identifying category shifts. These were all, in their own way, engine-building projects.

To build engines is to treat certain capabilities, such as pricing, risk, logistics, triage, and engagement, as ongoing systems that can be improved, measured, and governed.

In practice, this might mean deciding as a leadership team that over the next three years, the organization will prioritize building, say, a world-class risk engine and a customer engagement engine. It might mean assigning clear ownership, investing in the necessary data and architecture, and integrating those engines into performance conversations. It might mean consciously deciding which engines to build internally and which to consume from national or corporate AI infrastructure.

The temptation will always be to chase the next shiny pilot. The discipline is to resist that temptation and keep returning to the question, 'Which engines define who we are in this ecosystem, and how are we making them better, month after month?'

A Different Kind of Strategy Conversation

These five disciplines—owning the interface, building identity graphs, governing at market speed, orchestrating ecosystems, and building engines—are deliberately framed as habits rather than one-time projects, and as questions for leadership, not technical prescriptions.

Taken together, they change the nature of the strategy conversation.

Instead of asking, 'What is our five-year digital roadmap?' leaders begin asking, 'Where are we likely to fracture if the AI-native environment described in this part arrives faster than we expect?' Instead of benchmarking digital features against peers, they challenge themselves to assess governance agility, data quality, and engine maturity. Instead of treating public digital infrastructure and national AI missions as an abstract context, they treat them as platforms they must learn to navigate.

In doing so, they become like the reinventors in Part IV: organizations that, often under pressure, chose to re-architect their businesses rather than decorate their legacy structures.

This is what it means to be future-ready, not with the possession of a particular technology or launch of a particular product but with the cultivation of organizational reflexes that allow leaders to see fault lines early, act before they crack the organization open and harness each technological wave for reinvention rather than decline.

The future described in this part—fast-growing, digital-heavy, AI-native, and shaped by India's infrastructure choices—will not be comfortable for everyone. Some enterprises will discover that their vulnerabilities run deeper than they thought. Others will find, to their surprise, that they are better positioned than they imagined, provided they move decisively.

The message to the reader is simple: you cannot slow the waves, but you can decide what kind of raft you are building.

At the Edge of What Comes Next

India's story has always unfolded in layers, quiet shifts beneath the surface, sudden ruptures above it, and long arcs of change that become clear only in hindsight. The journeys in this book reflect that rhythm. They show companies rising and falling, industries reorganizing themselves, and leaders learning, sometimes painfully, that disruption in India is neither an event nor a threat. It is the environment.

The cases, frameworks, and reflections shared here point towards a simple but demanding truth: Indian enterprises succeed or stumble not because of technology alone but because of their ability to recognize and respond to the deeper fault lines shaping the country. These fault lines of governance, behaviour, architecture, and adaptability move quietly at first, then overwhelmingly. Those who read them early gain time. Those who ignore them lose it.

This book grew out of a long personal journey of watching India rebuild itself again and again, first through liberalization, then through the spread of IT services and now through the rapid emergence of platforms, digital public infrastructure, and AI. To have lived through so many versions of the same country is a privilege as well as a responsibility. It reminds us that the India we inhabit today is not a finished design but a work in progress. It also reminds us that leadership in such a landscape cannot depend on certainty. It must depend on curiosity, imagination, and the willingness to question what appears stable.

The predictions and foresight exercises in this book are intentionally risky. Some may be proven right, others may not. That is beside the point. They are included to encourage the reader to embrace ambiguity as a strategic asset. In a nation as dynamic as ours, accuracy is temporary, whereas the ability to think expansively is enduring.

If there is one message that threads through every chapter, it is that the ground will continue to shift. Platforms will evolve. AI will redraw boundaries. Consumer behaviour will accelerate. Governance models will stretch and strain. The firms that endure will not be the ones with the most resources but the ones with the clearest eyes and quickest feet, the ones that learn to move with the country rather than resist its momentum.

That brings this book to its final purpose.

India does not need leaders who wait for clarity. It needs leaders who are willing to create it. It needs leaders who examine their assumptions before circumstances do it for them, redesign their organizations before fault lines widen, and see disruption not as a storm to outlast but as a climate to understand.

As you step into the next phase of your journey as a founder, policymaker, board member, or industry leader, the invitation is simple: stay alert to the tremors beneath your feet, stay open to the questions you cannot yet answer, and stay willing to reinvent before reinvention becomes unavoidable.

The next chapter of India's economic story is already being written. It will reward those who act early, think deeply, and lead with imagination.

The call to action is to read the fault lines, embrace the ambiguity, and shape the future before it arrives.

Appendix A

Fault Line Executive Workshop™

A One-Day Leadership Alignment Programme

Objective

Enable leadership teams to identify vulnerabilities, detect emerging disruptions and prioritize resilience-building actions.

Session 1: Understanding the Fault Line Economy

Duration: 45 minutes

Activities:

- Review major disruption patterns
- Discuss industry shifts
- Align on disruption risks

Output:

Shared understanding

Session 2: Fault Line Fragility Index™

Duration: 90 minutes

Activities:

- Individual scoring
- Team scoring
- Debate differences

Output:

Fragility profile

Session 3: Identify Strategic Signals
Duration: 90 minutes
Activities:
Identify signals across:

- Customer drift
- Interface erosion
- Platform encroachment
- Technology substitution
- Regulatory realignment

Output:
Signal inventory

Session 4: Signal Scoring
Duration: 60 minutes
Score every signal against:

- Velocity
- Spread
- Inevitability

Output:
Top strategic threats

Session 5: Dashboard Construction
Duration: 60 minutes
Score all 10 dashboard drivers.

Output:
Fault Line Heat Map™

Session 6: Strategic Response Design
Duration: 90 minutes

Identify:

- Top 3 vulnerabilities
- Top 3 opportunities
- Top 3 no-regret moves

Output:
Fault Line Action Plan

Appendix B

Worked Example

Applying the Fault Line System™ to a Retail Bank

Consider a hypothetical mid-sized retail bank. The bank is profitable. The branch network remains strong. Customer satisfaction remains healthy. Traditional metrics suggest stability. The Fault Line Framework reveals a different story.

Step 1

Fragility Index™

Dimension	Score
Governance capability	18/25
Digital core strength	10/25
Business model resilience	15/25
Leadership foresight	17/25

Total: 60/100

Interpretation

Watch Zone

Performance remains healthy. Vulnerabilities are emerging. The greatest weakness is Digital Core Strength.

Step 2

Signal Radar™

Leadership identifies three signals.

Signal 1: AI Financial Advisors

Filter	Score
Velocity	5
Spread	4
Inevitability	5

Total = 14
Action Required

Signal 2: Digital-Only Banking

Filter	Score
Velocity	4
Spread	5
Inevitability	5

Total = 14
Action Required

Signal 3: Open Banking Ecosystems

Filter	Score
Velocity	3
Spread	4
Inevitability	5

Total = 12
Prepare

Step 3
Dashboard™

Driver	Score
Governance agility	4
Digital core strength	2
Business model elasticity	3
Leadership foresight	4
Platform threat exposure	2
Customer migration velocity	2
Regulatory and infrastructure realignment	3
Technology modernization speed	2
Capital reallocation agility	4
Ecosystem playmaking capability	2

Step 4
Heat Map Findings
Critical Exposure Areas:

Digital core
Platform exposure
Customer migration
Technology speed
Ecosystem capability

Step 5
No-Regret Moves

1. Modernize customer data architecture.
2. Launch AI-enabled relationship management.
3. Build ecosystem partnerships.
4. Reduce dependence on branch-centric customer acquisition.
5. Establish Quarterly Fault Line Reviews™.

Acknowledgements

To Shivkumar ('Shiv'), a friend and business partner for over 20 years.

Through seasons of risk, reinvention, and reflection, he has been both a counsel and a compass. He read this manuscript with patience, challenged its arguments with clarity, and encouraged me quietly but firmly to give it my best.

Every serious endeavour benefits from a steady mind beside it.

To Judhajit Das ('Jit'), my schoolmate and friend of four decades.

His kindness has always been quiet, his maturity steady, and his equanimity unwavering. In moments of doubt or intensity, his clarity of thought has pushed me to sharpen my own. His intellectual depth challenges me, and his leadership reminds me that strength and grace can coexist.

Some friendships evolve. Ours has endured and elevated.